PAINTING AND LINING MODEL LOCOMOTIVES AND COACHES

PAINTING AND LINING MODEL LOCOMOTIVES AND COACHES

GEOFF HAYNES

THE CROWOOD PRESS

DEDICATION

This book is dedicated to my parents, Rosemary and Peter. It was my dad who first got me into modelling, helping me to select tools and my first airbrush, just after my 10th birthday. It was my mum who allowed the kitchen to become a spraying area, and for modelling – including painting – to take place in the lounge.

ACKNOWLEDGEMENTS

This book would not have been possible without the excellent photographic skills of Tony Wright. On no fewer than six occasions, he came to my work room and spent the majority of the day photographing various models in progress. He also did 10 photo sessions for me in his studio. For this I thank him sincerely.

I must also thank my brother Ivan, who proofread my workings, and was constantly available to bounce off ideas throughout the writing process.

My thanks also go to Alan Brackenborough, whom I have known for as long as I can remember, as he is a friend of my parents. Alan represents the benchmark in model painting and is probably the most revered professional model painter in the business. I have early memories of watching him spraying in his basement and painting in his work room, which had a particularly memorable and (to me at least) pleasant smell of turps. His table was normally full of models, each at a different stage of painting. He has been a point of reference and advice over the years, both before and after I turned professional.

The late Alan Browning was a major influence on my early years in railway modelling. With an eye for detail, he inspired me to identify the variances between locomotives of the same class, and showed me how to model that detail.

Finally, I thank Sue my partner, and our two daughters Joanna and Abbey, for their support while I was writing this book.

CHAPTER ONE

INTRODUCTION

I have always wanted to paint my own models. I first started spray-painting at the age of 10 with the old Humbrol airbrush. After a trip to the Farnborough Airshow, I received a number of plastic aircraft kits for my 10th birthday, and my dad encouraged me to spend some of my birthday money on some paint, and on that airbrush. My pocket money would not stretch to the cans available for the supply of air, so we obtained a car wheel and tyre and used that for the purpose. Having then got into modelling ex-Midland LMS, I built up a small collection of plain matt black liveried locomotives and one black loco, which was lined by my dad. After a few years, I felt it was time to upgrade my airbrush, and I bought a Paasche, along with a simple compressor. Feeling brave, I had a go at a crimson loco, which I lined to

RIGHT: **My first commission, photographed on the client's layout. The loco is a GWR Bulldog, from a Martin Finney kit.** PAUL BASON

BELOW: **The LNER Silver Jubilee train, photographed on Tony Wright's layout of Little Bytham. The coaches are built from Marc Models kits and the loco is a repainted Hornby model, supplied by the client.**

a reasonable standard with Rotring-type pens and water-based paint. I then built a number of coaches that needed lining in LMS livery, and achieved success again with the Rotring pens. However, I realized that, in order to get the range of colours I needed for other liveries and to obtain more consistent performance, I would need to develop my skills with a bow pen. I also upgraded my compressor to a larger model, this time with a reservoir. I started to spray finishes that were not just matt and it was at this point I realized that my technique was not correct. After a lot of practice and research, I worked out what I was doing wrong and was able to change my approach.

The first model that I built as a commission was back in 2004. I was to paint the chassis mainframes satin black, and then return the reassembled model for painting by someone else. It felt strange to me to be letting go a part-completed model. I completed three commissions in total to this specification. By 2006, I was introduced to someone who wanted a GWR Bulldog built for his OO layout. This relationship developed, and I ended up building two more locos for him in O gauge, and then painting and lining a GWR King, an auto coach, a Banana railcar, and a pair of B set coaches, all in O gauge. I continued to take a very small number of complete build and paint commissions over subsequent years, fitting them between the day job and my own modelling. In the spring of 2014, I decided that I would make the model-making my day job. My intention was to provide a building service that included painting, lining and weathering to clients' specifications. However, as word has spread, I have taken in a number of painting and lining, and also weathering, commissions, which I am fitting in and around the building jobs.

This book aims to cover all the main areas of painting railway models, including the preparation, which actually goes back to the building part of the process, the priming and the main colours. Then I will look at ways to apply lining to models, with step-by-step photos. The application of lettering, numbering and decals comes next; I always get the lining done before applying decals, as lining is generally by far the longer job and I want to minimize the risk of damage to transfers by handling. Occasionally, I have been unhappy with a result and have decided to start over. In such cases, if I had already put the transfers on, they would have been lost. On the other hand, if a transfer needs to be removed, it is easy to do this with no damage to the paint underneath. The next stage is varnishing, then in the last chapter I will take a brief look at the weathering process.

An O gauge Bachmann Brassworks King, painted and lined for the same client as the Bulldog – my first attempt at lining in 7mm scale.

My own Duchess of Sutherland, built from a Martin Finney kit, seen on my O gauge garden line. The coaches were built by Brian Flanagan.

CHAPTER TWO

TOOLS FOR THE JOB

Part of the process of making models, whichever outline you choose, is painting. For some, it is the highlight of a project; for others, it is a chore. What is certain is that, as the paint is applied, a model really starts to come to life.

BRUSHING OR SPRAYING?

There are a number of approaches to painting. The first decision is whether to brush-paint or to spray. I prefer to spray as much as possible, and to avoid brush-painting of anything other than very small areas. I feel that I can obtain a better finish with an airbrush. Unlike many other professional model painters, I will always spray buffer beams, for example. I have never been happy with brush-painting these, but this does mean that I am faced with some time-consuming and tricky masking situations.

Spraying can be done from a can or by using an airbrush. Some manufacturers supply model paint in spray cans, but, rather than using the can to apply the paint, I prefer to transfer it into a jar, adjust the thinning, and then spray the paint through an airbrush. I have used cans of car paint to spray directly on to a model – normally a primer and very occasionally a top coat – but I much prefer having the control afforded by spraying through an airbrush. The surface of a model is not always flat; it can have internal corners and items of detail can create shadows. Using an airbrush allows the painter to vary the amount of paint to suit these situations.

If a model requires lining, this can be achieved with either transfers or paint. I have come across two types of lining transfer: Pressfix and waterslide, which will be covered in more detail later on. There is a specific lining pen available, often seen at exhibitions, but it will not paint lines thin enough for the smaller scales. Painting with Rotring-type pens is relatively easy, but the flow of paint is rather inconsistent over time, and each pen will only deliver one thickness of line. Lining with bow pens is probably the most common, but it does take some preparation and practice.

TOOLS FOR SPRAYING

When I first started spraying models in my youth, I powered my airbrush with a car tyre mounted on a wheel (an inner tube alone lacked the necessary power). Needless to say, the pressure was never constant, as the tyre was always deflating itself, but it was acceptable for what I was doing then. I still have a couple of models that were sprayed using the car tyre and my old Humbrol airbrush. I did have an air canister, but only one; knowing that this would cost pocket money to replace, I never actually used it.

I have since then had experience with two types of compressor. I bought a Rotring compressor at the same time as my Paasche airbrush. Again, this worked fine, but there was a feeling of the air

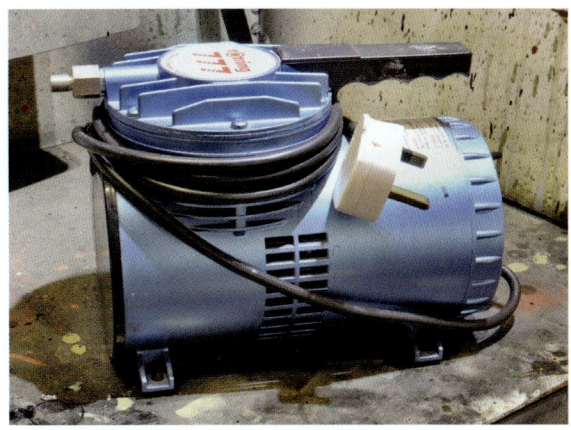

My first compressor. It has no reservoir of air, so runs constantly, and it delivers air with a pulse rather than a constant flow.

pulsing as it emitted from the airbrush. There can of course be no substitute for a compressor with its own reservoir, complete with a moisture trap, and a pressure control valve. This allows you to regulate the air pressure of each airbrush, and according to each type of paint, and be assured of a steady pulse and a free flow of air. It is vital to keep an eye on the pressure, however, as some spray jobs can easily use more than one tank full. It is possible to get around this by leaving the compressor switched on, so that, when the pressure in the tank gets down to a certain level, the compressor will recharge it. It does tend to make you jump out of your skin when you are concentrating hard on a complex job and the compressor suddenly comes back to life. With this compressor, as the pressure in the tank starts to get low, the regulated output connected to my airbrush seems to increase. If I have not at that point already noticed that the pressure is getting low, this serves as a prompt.

This type of equipment need not be expensive. My compressor was an Aldi 'special buy' a number of years ago, and came with a number of other accessories, including a spray gun and a tyre inflator for my car, all for about £50. I have seen similar offers over the years, and this type of compressor also appears in tool retailers' catalogues.

I no longer have my original Humbrol airbrush. The air valve started leaking after a number of years and I felt it was time to upgrade to something a little more serious. The various types of airbrush include internal mix and external mix. The external-mix airbrush is the rather more basic model, which works by way of the air blowing across the nozzle at the top of the paint container. The flow of paint is controlled by the height of the nozzle. As the name implies, with the internal-mix airbrush, the mixing of the air and paint occurs inside the tool. The flow of paint is controlled by a needle valve inside the

My current compressor. Similar examples are available from various tool suppliers for a reasonable price. This one came with a number of attachments, including a spray gun (a little too big for model painting), an air line, and a tyre inflator. It saves paying to use the air line at the local petrol station!

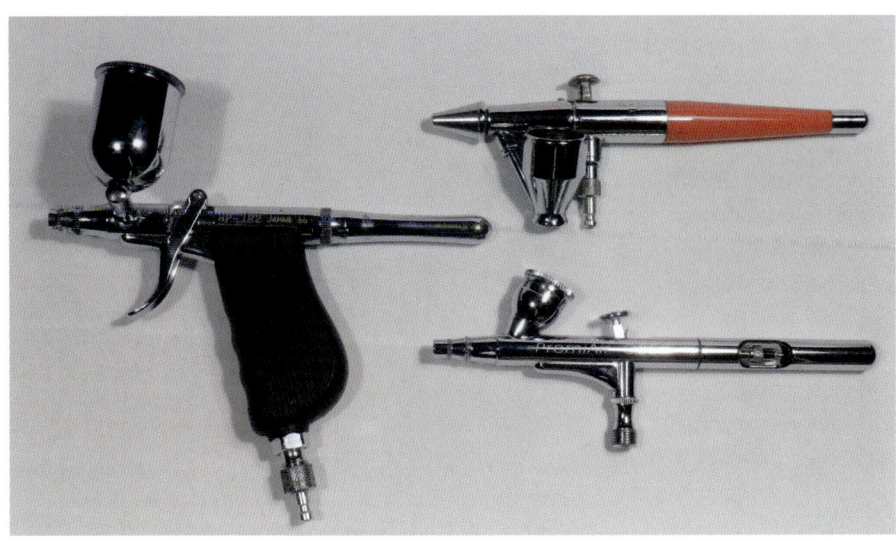

My fleet of three airbrushes: (top right) the Paasche VL; (underneath) the PremiAir G35; and (left) the Iwata TR2.

TOOLS FOR THE JOB 11

The spray booth is made of hardboard and the fan fits on to ducting that goes out through an external wall. All the components for this project were bought from a local DIY store for a few pounds.

Looking upwards at my spray booth lighting, simply a household low-voltage light set with some daylight LED bulbs. Each lamp can be positioned easily by hand.

airbrush. Airbrush types are further divided into single-action and dual-action. With a single-action airbrush, the button operates just the air, switching it on and off. The needle inside the needle valve can be moved by a separate control, normally at the back of the airbrush. This means that the flow of paint is constant whilst you are spraying. With a dual-action airbrush, the button or trigger operates the air flow in the same way as a single-action airbrush, but, as the button is moved backwards, first the air is switched on, then the paint is gradually introduced. The further the button is moved back, the more paint is emitted.

Once you have spraying equipment, you also need somewhere to use it. I used to spray in the kitchen, taking the time to lay out plenty of newspaper first, then giving the room a good airing afterwards. Now, I have a room dedicated to model-making – an

Both my lights came from The Craft Light company. The large main light is the LED Adjusta lamp, 1500 lumen 12-watt, and has four settings of brightness. The smaller lamp on the left has a high-definition 6-watt LED bulb, which provides a very strong localized beam that has to be seen to be appreciated.

12 | TOOLS FOR THE JOB

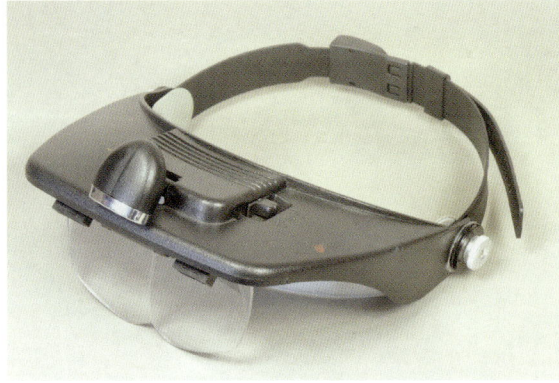

I wear glasses for reading and model-making, but I need further magnification when lining. This device comes with four different magnifying lenses.

integral garage, which was converted into a spare room a number of years ago. My spraying area is set up in one corner. The spray booth is simply three pieces of hardboard fitted together and painted white. (It does not stay white for very long, so every so often it is whitewashed again.) There is a fan fitted in a hole in the back piece of hardboard, connected to some ducting that goes to an external wall. It is very important to have an extraction system when working with cellulose paint and thinners, to avoid inhaling the potentially harmful fumes. You should also have dedicated lighting for the spray booth or spraying area, as it is imperative to be able to see clearly how paint lands on the surface being painted.

Even though I use an extractor fan, I strongly recommend the wearing of a mask. My mask came from the catalogue of one of the many DIY and tool supplier chains.

TOOLS FOR LINING

I now exclusively use bow pens for painting lines on models. A long time ago, I used Rotring-type pens with paint, and these are still available from some suppliers. The advantage with the Rotring-type pen is that it is relatively easy to use and produces a consistent line. However, over time, despite keeping the pens clean and flushing through with cleaning fluid after use, they are prone to blocking. Also, each pen can only produce one width of line. Even though it is possible to paint thicker lines by repeating a line adjacent to the line just painted, this is not always practical. As a result, you need a number of pens in order to achieve the variety of line thicknesses required. I had two or three pens in the tool kit, giving line thicknesses of 0.13mm, 0.25mm and 0.5mm.

Today, I have two bow pens in regular use. One is a general pen that I bought from new from an art and stationery supplier some 30 years ago. I cannot recall the actual price, but it was significantly less than £5. It has needed some work to be able to produce the narrow lines that I require; for more on the detail of this work, see later. An added

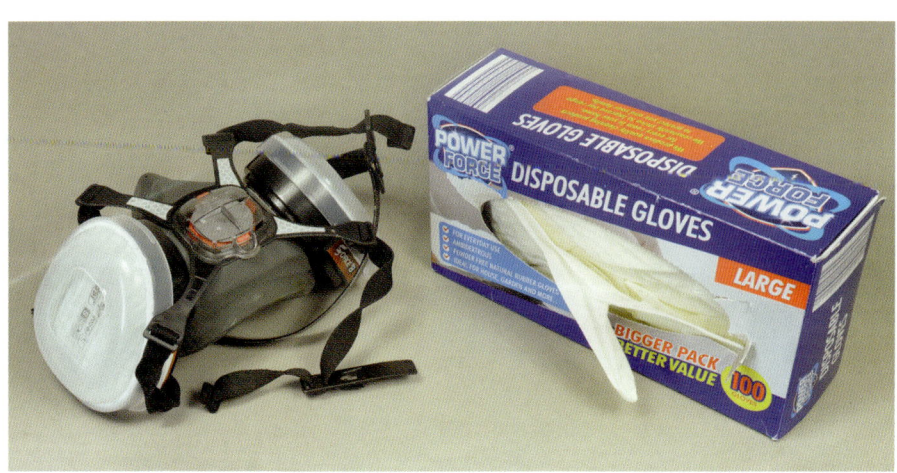

Even with an extractor fan, I still use a face mask whilst spraying. I also use a rubber glove on my left hand, which is the one I use to hold the model.

TOOLS FOR THE JOB

I have two bow pens in regular use for lining, and two very fine high-quality brushes.

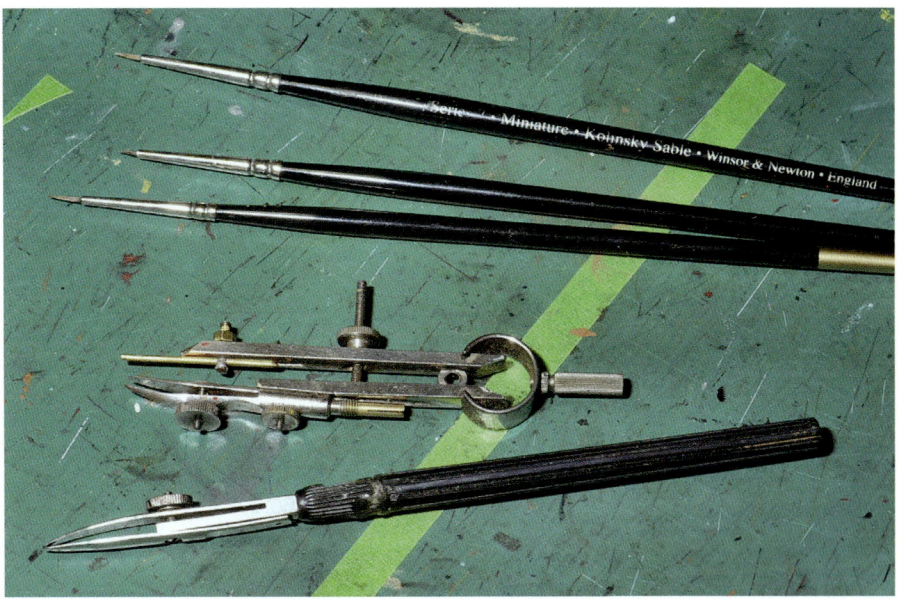

advantage of this pen is that one of the blades pivots, which makes cleaning so much easier. I am not sure where my other bow pen came from. My dad spent some time working as a draughtsman, many years ago, and I came across this pen in a box of bits. I then found a way of fitting it to a set of compasses, for use in painting curves.

Also needed for lining are some high-quality paintbrushes. I have two Winsor and Newton series 7 brushes, size 000 and 00, which are used for painting the curves that join vertical lines and horizontal lines. I also have some similar fine brushes (but perhaps less expensive) for tidying work after lines and curves have been painted. These are also used on the relatively few occasions when I brush-paint areas.

Finally, lining requires some decent lighting and some magnification. My lights come from a specialist supplier of lighting, The Craft Light Company. As with many people, middle age has brought on a degree of long-sightedness and a need for some additional assistance, along with my reading/modelling glasses. This magnifying visor comes with four levels of magnification; I use the second level. It also comes with an LED light, but I find it too small. With my main working lights (I use both when lining), I have sufficient light.

TOOLS FOR VARNISHING AND WEATHERING

You do not need much more equipment for varnishing and weathering than you already have for painting and lining. Varnish is applied by spraying, and weathering can be achieved either by spraying or brushing, more likely by a combination of both. However, it is certainly worth having a specific set of brushes for weathering, rather than using those that you have for lining and general brush-painting. This is because weathering can be rather harsher on your expensive front-line brushes. Other than that, in recent years an extensive range of weathering products has emerged, giving you a difficult choice to make.

Finally, there are two other 'tools' that you will need in abundance: patience and practice. I hope that the subsequent chapters will give you some inspiration and confidence to take your own modelling a step or two further.

CHAPTER THREE

PREPARATION

When painting, and particularly when spraying, the job is made more manageable if the surface to be painted is as flat as possible, and without corners to spray into or adjacent surfaces to catch overspray. Whilst the side of a coach is relatively flat and simple, a steam locomotive is quite the opposite, with corners at the places where parts fit to the footplate and where the firebox meets the cab. Items of detail create shadow areas, which can prevent sprayed paint landing in the right place on the area behind. A large proportion of a locomotive is far from flat.

In an ideal world, preparation for the painting stage would start early on in the building process. In terms of a locomotive, it might be expected that the chassis would be removable from the body. However, this surprisingly is not always the case, with some chassis parts being permanently fitted to the body. Even when the chassis can be removed from the body, it may not come apart far enough. The next question is whether the body can be dismantled into any sub-assemblies, and how far the coaches can be prised apart.

THE BUILDING STAGE

COACHES

Generally, there are three ways that coaches can be dismantled:

1. The roof can be permanently attached to the body, and the body can be removed from the underframe.
2. The roof can be removable from the body, and the body permanently attached to the underframe.
3. The roof can be removable from the body, and in turn the body can be removed from the underframe. From a painting perspective, this is the best arrangement.

RTR coaches have a removable roof and underframe. On some coaches, the roof and underframe are separate, however the body without a roof or underframe needs careful handling, as it can be weak. I have also built coaches with a fixed roof in situations where a removable roof would not provide the best all-round fit to the body. Finally, I have been presented with coaches to paint that have a removable roof and a fixed underframe. This is the least manageable arrangement, as it is easier to mask the roof than the underframe.

Whilst considering the build of the coach body, its strength is greatly enhanced if any partitions are built into the sides, but this means that either

Dismantling coaches on a ready-to-run model.

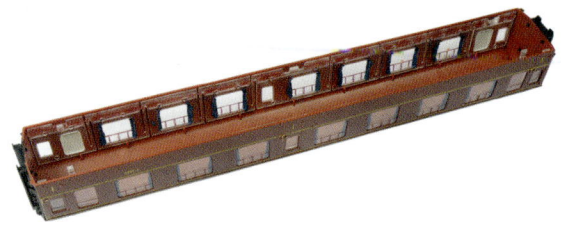

This coach separates from the underframe. Glazing is attached as units and clipped into place. On this example, the roof is part of the body shell.

PREPARATION 15

One of my painting commissions, this restaurant triple set is now running on its owner's layout.

The first class restaurant car shown dismantled. The body separates from the underframe, but the roof is permanently fixed to the body. The result is a very strong shell, with access to the interior, and no underframe to mask, as that is painted separately. An added bonus is a removable interior, which again makes painting easier.

Part of the next batch for painting, this buffet coach has been built with the body permanently fixed to the underframe, and with a separate roof. Once it has been primed, the body will be painted first, then, when fully dried, it will be masked to allow the underframe to be painted.

As well as being fixed to the underframe, this coach from the same batch also has a fitted interior. This will require some careful painting with a brush, but access is rather more restricted than if it was removable.

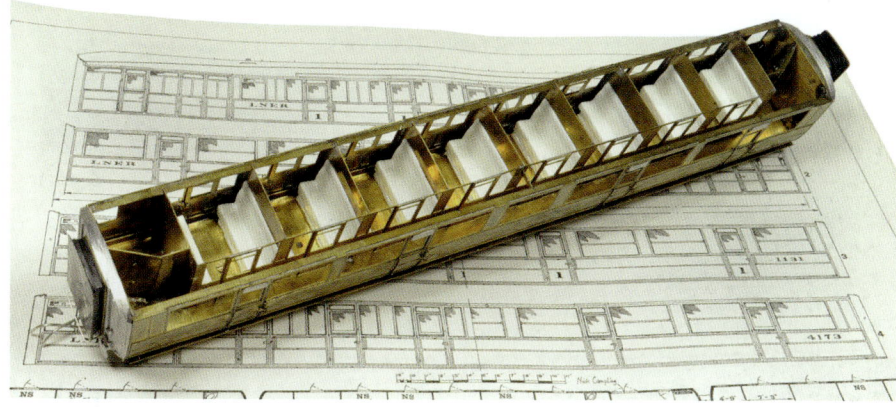

16 PREPARATION

I built these coaches some years ago from a pair of Comet kits.

These come apart to the fullest extent. The roof clips in at one end, then is bolted in at the brake end through the floor.

the coach interior is more difficult to paint, or any further detail (seating, and so on) needs to be painted first then added later.

In terms of the underframe, I would normally expect the bogies to be removable, but not wheel sets.

LOCOMOTIVE CHASSIS

The majority of locos that come to me for painting separate into two main parts: the body and the chassis. The chassis may disassemble slightly further, with bogies, pony trucks and sometimes wheel sets being removable, although the latter depends on the type of wheels and hornblocks used, and the scale of the model.

If the model has a compensated or sprung chassis, then some or all of the wheel sets would probably be removable out of the bottom of the chassis. If I am building the model myself, I would remove the wheels from the fixed axle, even though it would mean re-quartering this pair of wheels. However, on reassembly, only that set of wheels would need re-quartering and, in addition, I use a GW wheel press and quartering tool, so quartering adjustments are minimal.

If the model has Markits wheels, these can be unscrewed for painting. O gauge wheels are a little simpler, as wheels are for the most part Slaters, and can be individually removed by unscrewing. The only other wheel type I have encountered in O gauge is the Alan Harris, which again is easily removed; the axles are in two parts held together with a taper pin.

I also make outside cylinders removable, either

PREPARATION

locating them in position by sliding into slots (as designed into some kits), or making them to be bolted into position. This allows the whole assembly to be painted evenly and avoids the potential problem of shadow areas on the chassis.

One of my regular painting clients prefers to paint the chassis himself. He brush-paints the frames and the wheels, on the basis that, once the chassis works properly, it should not be disturbed. He works on the principle that, if it performs perfectly before disassembly, then the best that can be achieved on reassembly is the same standard, or just as likely a lower one.

Another OO loco that came to me for painting had a brush-painted chassis, but unpainted wheels and brake gear. This loco had full outside Walscherts valve gear and the crank pins were soldered in position. I decided to mask the chassis with slips of paper cut to fit either side of the axle, and just sliding in behind the wheels. It was then possible to brush-paint the valve gear, or polish it back to bare metal, after the wheels had been sprayed.

If the wheels need lining, I would want them to be completely removed from the chassis, ideally with coupling rods removed too.

LOCOMOTIVE BODY

The fact that the body is one assembly is not a problem. However, if I am building a locomotive, in most cases I will try to build the model so that it can be dismantled into a number of sub-assemblies, particularly if it is not destined to be painted just in black.

First, the firebox backhead is either glued or screwed in. The boiler being removable certainly aids the painting process, and also greatly simplifies the masking. Any smoke deflectors can be made to fit on after painting. If the model is a tank locomotive, then a removable roof will help, unless the cab details can be removed from the underside of the model. If it is a tender locomotive, ideally the underframe can be separated from the tank. Areas of detail on the footplate such as lubricators are best left off and painted separately, then either glued or screwed in place afterwards, as these restrict access to the underside of the boiler.

With the mainframes already painted with enamels by the builder, some protection is needed to paint the wheels.

Whilst I could have removed the wheels, this would have necessitated unsoldering the crankpin retention.

Another slip of paper will protect the pick-ups whilst the brake rodding is sprayed.

18 PREPARATION

THREE LOCOMOTIVE CASE STUDIES

WANTAGE TRAMWAY NUMBER 5

The Wantage Tramway Number 5, one of my 7mm scale scratch builds, seems to generate more interest than any of my other models. The advantage of a scratch-built model is that you do not have to adhere to the original instructions for a kit, or have to modify a kit to enable the building of sub-assemblies. On this one, the cab sides locate into a slot inside the cab front, and the bottom of the handrail stanchion then fits into a locating hole in the footplate. Each one is then secured with a 10BA bolt. The handrail bends at 90 degrees at the front to attach behind the cab side. This is barely visible once the sub-assembly is fitted. Not only did this facilitate the painting of the interior of the cab, it also made the hand lettering on the sides considerably easier.

The firebox surround and rear were glued into place after painting. The brass and copper top of the dome are two separate castings, and were also glued in place after painting. The whole chimney is a copper casting, and the top was polished after painting. The tool box and sand box are also secured to the footplate by a bolt. This removes potential obstructions in the spraying process.

I am currently building another of these locos for a client, and I intend to make the boiler a separate sub-assembly.

LMS DUCHESS OF SUTHERLAND

This model was completed a few years ago now and was used to try out a few skills and operations, including a number of sub-assemblies in construction, and the more complex LMS lining of red–gold–red–black.

All of the tender wheel sets can be removed, with the water pick-up assembly held in place with a 12BA bolt. The spring and axle-box castings were glued on after painting, which is always the ideal method if the tender frames are not black.

The cylinder and motion bracket assembly is removable, locating in slots from above and held in position with four 10BA bolts. In order to lift this, however, the linkage to the inside valve motion needs to be removed.

Another of my own models, a scratch-built locomotive in O gauge.

The locomotive body disassembles into a number of components, to facilitate the painting process.

PREPARATION | 19

One of my favourite models, the Duchess, built from a Martin Finney kit in O gauge.

The chassis was primed and painted black, then the outside was masked, and the inside was sprayed first with a red oxide primer, then vermillion. The leaf springs were built as another sub-assembly, allowing access to remove the wheel sets.

I normally try to make boilers removable if the model is not just black, but, whilst building this model, I found I had an opportunity to make the cab removable. The firebox backhead is bolted in position and, unusually, I opted to make the cab roof removable too. It clips into place at the back and is secured in place with a couple of bolts from inside the firebox. This decision came about more from a constructional point of view, to facilitate the fitting of the firebox backhead, than from a painting perspective. The smoke deflectors have 14BA threaded rod fitted to the bottom edge which locate in the footplate. The tops clip on to the handrails.

As well as the tank separating from the underframe, the tender chassis is also removable.

The cylinders and motion bracket is made as a removable sub-assembly; the bolts holding this in place are clearly visible.

20 PREPARATION

The body of this model comes apart into a number of sub-assemblies.

Clearly visible here are the nuts holding on the various lubricators and oil reservoirs.

Viewed from the top, the detail is visible.

PREPARATION

GWR CASTLE

The Castle was built from a Malcom Mitchell kit, which required very little modification to arrive at the various sub-assemblies. On the body, the boiler assembly screws in place through the cab into the firebox, and through the footplate into the smokebox.

I made the brake gear as a separate unit in my normal way. The chassis was built as compensated, so the front and centre driving wheels drop out

Straight from the workbench, and prior to cleaning, a late Castle, built from a Malcolm Mitchell kit.

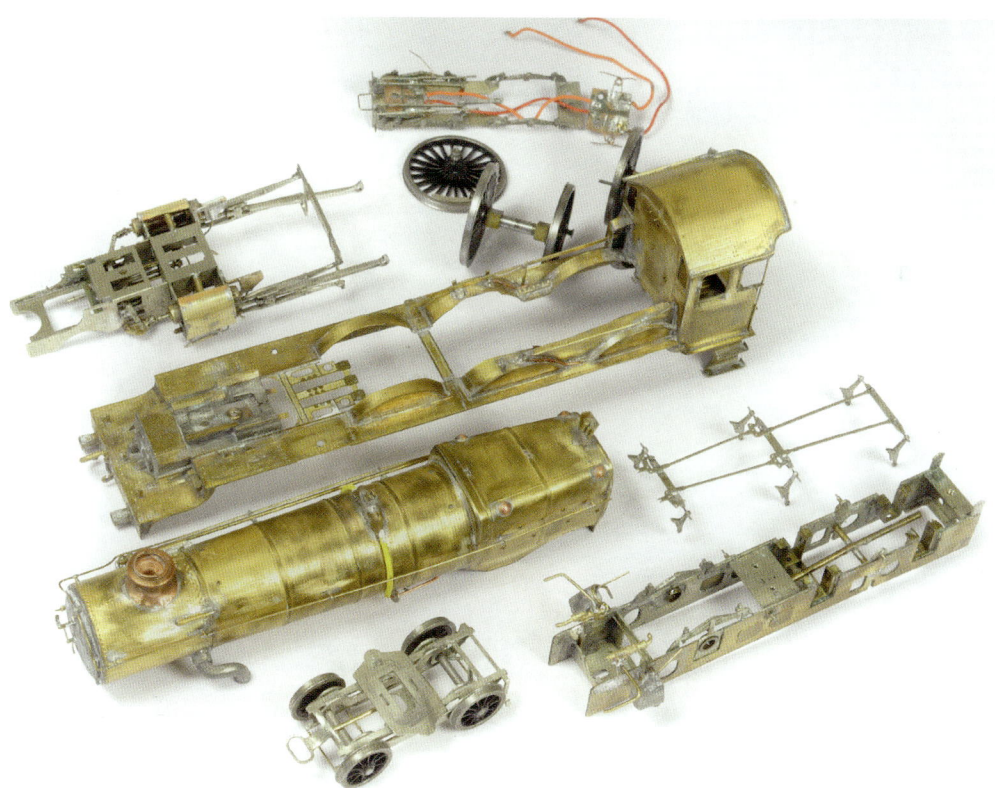

The Castle dismantled for cleaning and then painting. The bogie wheels will also be removed.

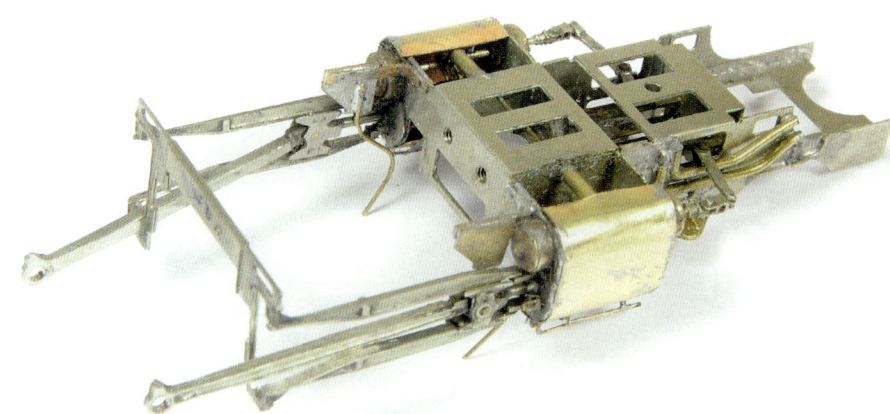

Slidebars and crossheads for the inside cylinders are built into the front of this assembly. These and the valves are driven by linkage from the outside cylinders.

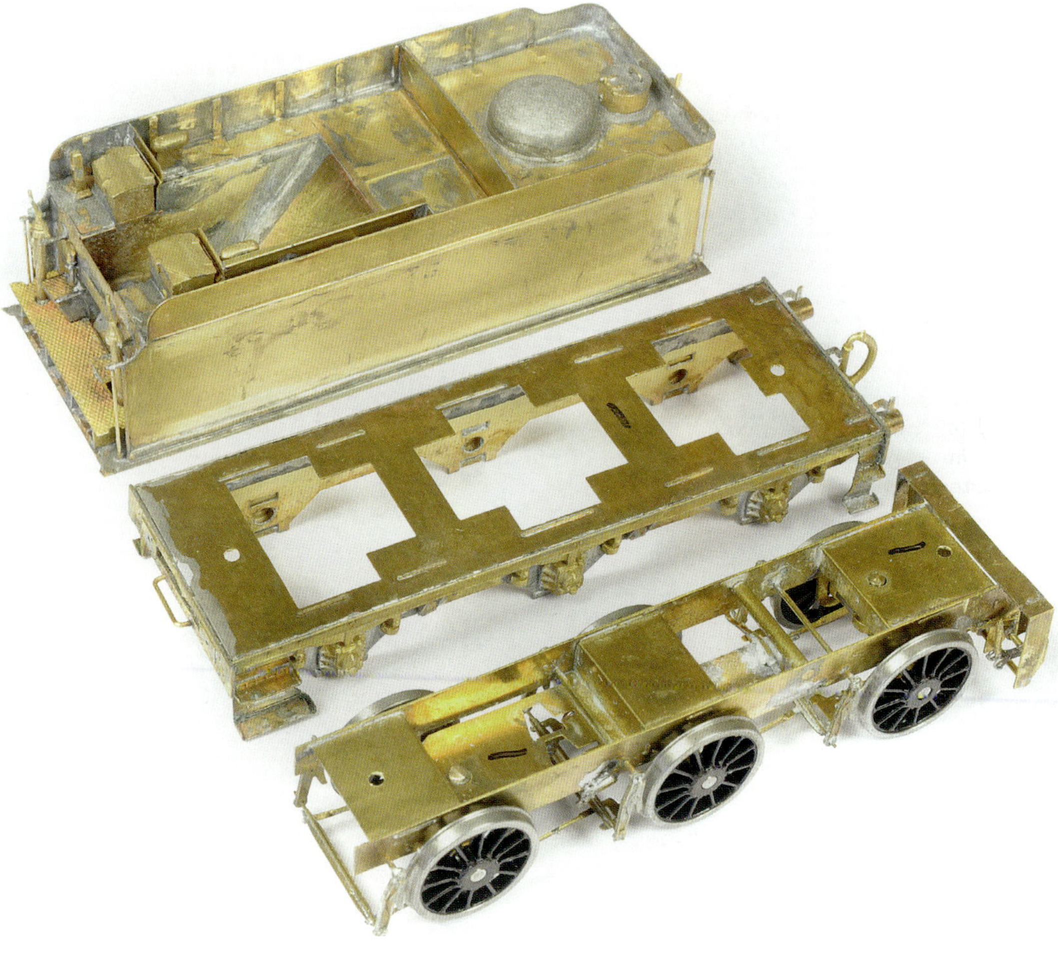

The three parts of the tender. Again, the tender wheels will be removed for cleaning and painting.

PREPARATION 23

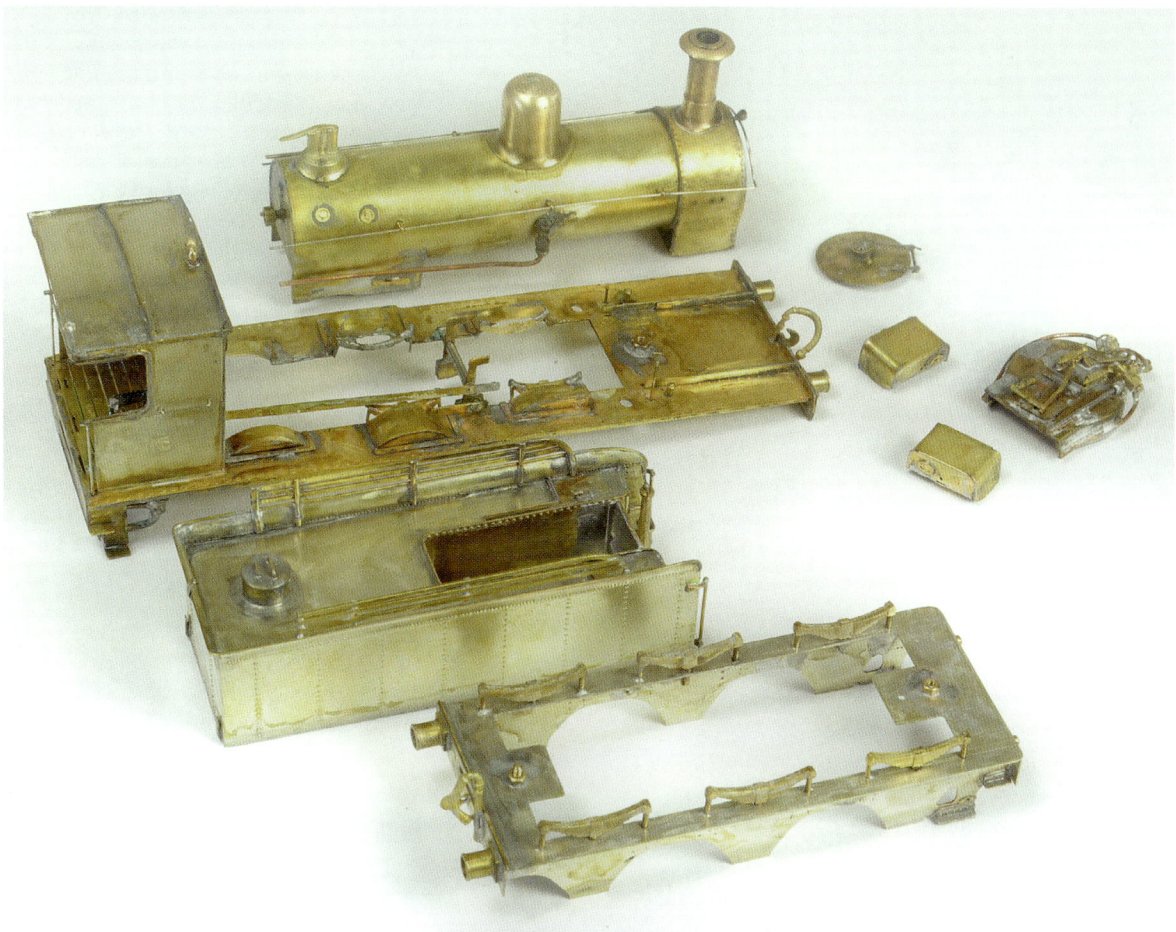

This model was passed to me for painting. The loco had been built with the boiler separating from the cab and footplate assembly, and the sand boxes were removable too. The smokebox door and the firebox backhead were attached with magnets. On the tender, which was built by someone else, the body separates from the underframe.

of their hornblocks. They are retained by the leaf springs, which are assembled as a unit with some of the brake rods and pick-ups.

The motion assembly separates from the mainframes, but what is unusual is that the whole front section of the frames is part of this sub-assembly. This is actually how the kit is designed, as it incorporates working inside crossheads, and valve linkage, and this is achieved most easily when all is incorporated into the same assembly. This section is secured to the front of the mainframes with two 10BA bolts.

The tender body separates from the underside in the conventional way, which simplifies the masking process. The underside consists of the main outer assembly and inside frames, which include the brake gear and water scoop detail.

PREPARING FOR PAINTING

Before the painting process can be undertaken, the whole model needs to be cleaned, with all traces of flux being removed. It then needs to be thoroughly degreased. This is the final chance to inspect

24 PREPARATION

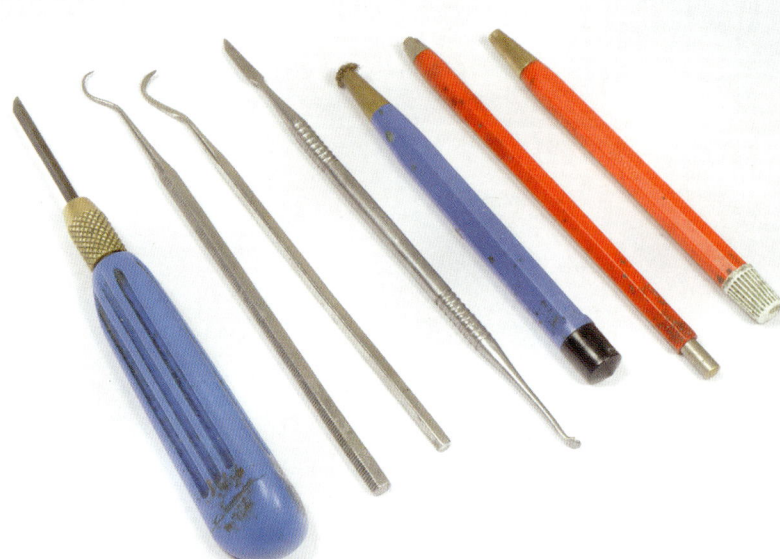

The scraper (left), kept sharp on a sharpening stone when required, is excellent for removing excess solder. The curved dental probes are ideal for reaching into difficult areas and behind items of detail. The burnishing tools (right) can be used to polish the surface, to ensure that the area is completely clean. They can often leave behind small fragments of fibreglass, which will either get into your fingers, or hide on the model surface, but the washing process normally takes care of this.

the model for any excess or stray solder. A random selection of scrapers, burnishing tools and dental probes will be ideal for digging out and polishing off any unwanted remnants of the building process.

A painter's worst nightmare at this point is a model built with paste flux. Any traces of stray flux that are not completely removed will act slowly as paint stripper. If you decide to build a model with paste flux, you need to be particularly diligent in removing all traces. Additionally, I have used enough solder to fill joints, so that there are no crevices where remnants of flux might hide. In more recent times I have switched to a liquid flux, which is much more easily and quickly cleaned off the model.

The washing process comes next. A wash in a solution that is slightly alkaline will help to neutralize any remaining flux, but be aware that concealed traces of paste flux can be immune to this part of the process. A simple household cleaner such as Flash should suffice. Give the model a good scrub with a paintbrush, or an old toothbrush (or a com-

The first part of the washing process: giving the model a good scrub with a simple household cleaner.

Again, the Viakal had an immediate effect on the tarnished surface of this rather old nickel silver tender.

Although the Viakal had an immediate effect on the etched brass tender side of this model, there is still some old paint on the frames. This will need to be removed before the model is resprayed.

bination of both, to ensure that you get well inside the model, and into any corners on the exterior). Clearly, care is needed when scrubbing around areas of detail, but if something is going to fall off, it is better that this happens before the painting has begun!

Immediately after the alkaline wash stage, repeat the process with a household limescale remover such as Viakal. This is slightly acidic, and will give a slight pickling effect on the surface of the brass or nickel silver. The next stage is a thorough rinse in water, under a running tap (put the plug in first, in case anything should fall off!), and then the model needs to be left to dry thoroughly. Put it in a drying box (a plant propagator makes a good one) and put this into the airing cupboard, preferably overnight. When the model is completely dry, brush over with some cellulose thinners, to give a final degrease. Allow it to dry again – this should not take long, as cellulose thinners evaporate quite quickly. From this point, the model should be handled as little as possible.

All traces of the two washes must be removed.

After the first scrub, the model is washed with limescale remover. Make sure you get into every corner.

CHAPTER FOUR

USING AN AIRBRUSH

CHOOSING YOUR AIRBRUSH

There are a number of types of airbrush available, but the two main categories are external-mix and internal-mix. The focus here will be on the internal-mix type, single-action or dual-action.

The Badger 200 series is one example of a single-action airbrush that is simple to use. When the air is switched on, by depressing the button on top, the amount of paint that is delivered is constant. That amount is effectively pre-set by the use of an adjuster at the back of the airbrush, which moves the needle forwards to reduce paint flow, and backwards to increase it. The Badger 200 airbrush is ideal for spraying simple areas, but where there are internal corners to spray into, handrails and other details to spray behind, the flow of paint needs to be reduced while spraying. Although this is easy to do by turning the adjuster on the back of the airbrush, it has to be done with the hand that is not holding the airbrush, and this does interrupt the flow of the painting.

The dual-action airbrush is so called because the button or trigger has two functions. It switches on the air and also controls the amount of paint flowing through. Whilst this may sound complex, with practice it can become almost second nature. When spraying around raised detail, behind handrails or into corners, less paint will be needed. Then, when you move on to the larger areas, the paint flow is easily increased by pulling back on the button or trigger.

I have three airbrushes, all dual-action. With the Paasche VL airbrush, paint is drawn up from a cup that fits into the bottom of the unit. The Iwata TR2 airbrush supplies paint from a cup that fits into the side of the airbrush. The PremiAir G35 is a top-feed airbrush, which has a cup that is integral to the main body of the tool. The Paasche is the oldest of my airbrushes, and for some time it did all of my spraying. Now, I tend to use it mainly for priming, particularly when using etch primers. Whilst I always clean my airbrushes after use, I prefer not to use these paints in my front-line airbrush.

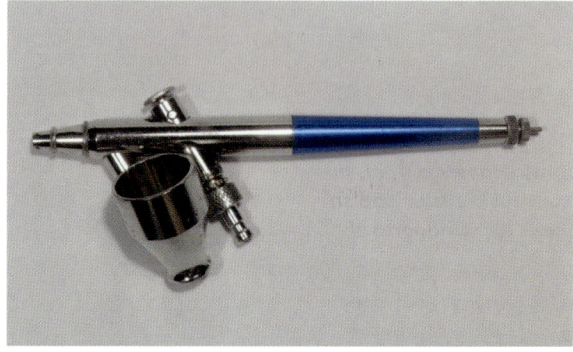

A single-action airbrush, where the screw adjustment on the rear dictates the amount of paint emitted. The trigger on the top is an on/off button for the air and the amount of paint flow is regulated solely by the rear adjuster.

For a long time, the Paasche VL was my only airbrush. It is a reliable tool, capable of producing an excellent finish and comes with three different needle/nozzle sizes. However, the vast majority of modelling applications require the largest needle.

USING AN AIRBRUSH

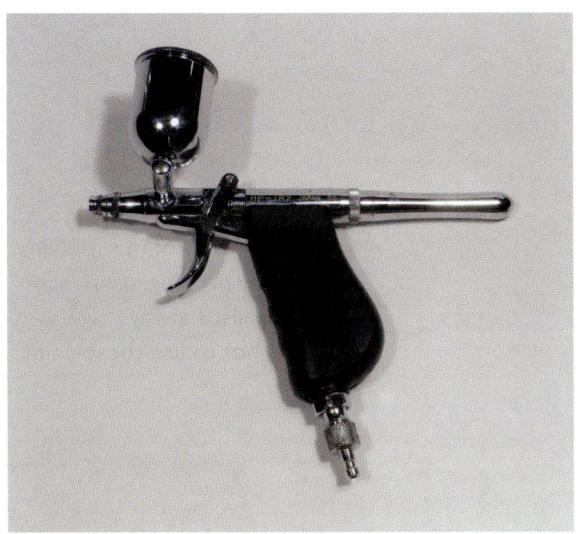

The feel of the Iwata airbrush is just different. It is comfortable to hold, and the air and paint flow is just much easier and smoother to control. Perhaps this is partly due to the underslung trigger, which, being longer, has a slight mechanical advantage.

I acquired the PremiAir as part of a magazine subscription offer a number of years ago. It is a perfectly good and very reasonably priced tool, although the size of the cup can be restricting in terms of larger spraying tasks. As a result, this airbrush does tend to remain in its box more often than not, although it did recently prove very useful during a weathering job. I had a weathering colour mixed in the Iwata airbrush and needed a matt wash, but had not finished with the weathering colour. It was very convenient to be able simply to reach for another airbrush, rather than having to empty and clean out the Iwata and start again.

The Iwata TR2 is a rather more expensive piece of engineering. When it was reviewed in the model press a few years ago, the writer sounded rather like a motoring journalist reviewing a top-of-the-range luxury car that he had particularly enjoyed driving. The article tempted me to give the model a try at an exhibition, and it was duly added to my tool kit.

An important consideration when choosing an airbrush is the spray width – that is to say, the width of paint that will be delivered in one pass. For model purposes, the general rule of thumb is the wider the band the better. The Paasche airbrush comes with three sizes of nozzle and three matching needles. It rarely has any but the largest nozzle fitted when I am using it. The Iwata TR2 has the widest spray band in this range of airbrushes. The general idea is to cover as much area as possible in as few passes as possible, as this will minimize the risk of the painted surface having the appearance of stripes.

It is possible at some exhibitions to try airbrushes before you buy them. Eileen's Emporium is one trader who offers this service, and is happy to offer advice on various aspects of spraying models.

VARIABLES IN SPRAYING

There are a number of variables that need to be taken into consideration when spraying: the ratio of paint to thinners; the ratio of air to paint; the air pressure; and the distance of the airbrush from the surface to be painted.

RATIO OF PAINT TO THINNERS

Most paints need to be thinned to some extent to be able to pass successfully through an airbrush. Otherwise, the airbrush will block. If the paint is not thinned sufficiently, it may pass through the airbrush, but will start to dry as it passes through the air, before landing on the surface to be painted. This will result in an uneven finish, similar to the outside of an orange. Appropriately enough, it is known as the 'orange peel effect', as the paint is starting to dry when it lands on the surface, so that it does not 'pool' sufficiently and dries unevenly in a series of peaks and troughs.

It is possible to counter the orange peel effect whilst the paint is still wet by spraying more paint on, preferably slightly thinner. The additional paint volume will flow into the peaks and troughs, and form a more even coat. Care must be taken, however, not to flood the surface with too much paint. This is one of those many times where practice will help.

If the paint has too much thinners, it will require

several coats to cover. This leads to the temptation to spray more on too soon, resulting in flooding and runs.

The ratio of paint to thinners will also vary according to the type of paint being sprayed. As a guide, cellulose paint will require a lot of thinners – in the region of one part paint to three parts thinners. Enamel and acrylic paints are generally one part paint to one part thinner. There are some exceptions. Railmatch paints, for example, generally state that the user should not exceed 20 per cent thinners when spraying, so the ratio works out as four parts paint to one part thinner.

RATIO OF AIR TO PAINT

This ratio is governed by the needle in the airbrush, and ultimately by the finger pulling back on the trigger. The flow of air through the airbrush is constant (depending on the compressor working correctly) and, in terms of air, the trigger is an on/off switch. The amount of paint required will vary depending on the part of the model that is being sprayed. If spraying into corners, inside cabs, or behind other items of detail, less paint is needed, so the trigger is not pulled back so far. For general spraying, larger amounts of paint are required

AIR PRESSURE

The ideal pressure for an airbrush is between 15 and 25 psi. Too little pressure, and the paint will not spray. Too much pressure, and the paint that has already been sprayed on to the surface will be blown around, damaging the finish. Thicker paint requires more air pressure. Similarly, an airbrush that feeds from the bottom (such as the Paasche VL) will need slightly more pressure, as it has to draw the paint up. Conversely, a side- or top-feed airbrush has the paint ready in the body of the tool. However, these variations are slight.

SPRAYING DISTANCE

It is surprising how close the airbrush can be to the surface, but the ideal distance varies according to what is being sprayed. General spraying will be 3–5cm from the surface of the model. When

GLOSS OR MATT?

Whilst the original mix of paint in a tin may appear constant in terms of the finish (matt, satin or gloss), the level of gloss or matt on a model can be varied slightly by two factors. First, the more thinners added to the paint prior to spraying, the glossier the finish. Second, the further the spraying distance, the more matt the finish. Understanding this second point is rather useful. If the level of gloss appears to be too much whilst you are spraying, a light spray over from further back, or even at a slight angle to the model, will tone it down. This is worth experimenting and practising with.

spraying a very specific area, such as behind a piece of detail, it may be necessary to spray closer than 1cm, but only a small amount of paint is required, so the trigger need only be pulled back slightly. If a weathering or toning wash is being applied, the distance would be further, perhaps 10cm or more.

BEFORE SPRAYING A MODEL

If you have just bought a new airbrush, it is important to get the feel of the flow of paint before you start spraying on models. Even if you are familiar with an airbrush, it is always advisable to test the flow of paint before moving to a model. I always have a small sheet of metal to hand on which to spray some paint. This allows me to check that the paint is landing properly on the surface, which means that the ratio of paint to thinners is correct. After a few passes with the airbrush, I also now have a piece of painted metal that will be useful in the lining process later.

SPRAYING

In terms of basic spraying, there are a few general points to make. First, do not start spraying whilst

USING AN AIRBRUSH | 29

One of my smaller test pieces – a spare strip of metal. Before attempting to put some paint on a model, it is worthwhile checking that the paint flows as it should, that the amount of paint emitted is as expected, and that it looks right as it lands on the surface.

As the paint goes on, I can see under my lights that the surface is wet, but that coverage is not quite complete. However, this first coat provides a good base to which more paint can be added in a few minutes, when it has dried.

the airbrush is pointing at the surface. Instead, start spraying whilst it is pointing to the side of the surface, then move the airbrush across. Nine times out of ten, there will be no problem, but, even with my experience, I have made this mistake. Every once in a while, the airbrush will not start cleanly, and some paint will spit. If the airbrush is pointing at the model, a number of paint spots will land on it. These will need to be rubbed down after drying and then another coat applied.

After the second coat has been applied, the wet surface can be seen. The colour is now covering evenly.

I have a number of sheets of metal that have been sprayed up and are then used for testing my bow pen, once it has been filled with paint. This is both to ensure that the paint is flowing properly, and to set it to the desired line width.

Whilst I was learning to spray, I used to think I had a valuable skill in being able to spray very thin coats, which did not seem to cause a problem whilst producing matt finishes. However, when I started trying to spray anything other than a matt finish, I found that the finish was far from acceptable. If any reflection is visible on a surface, any slight imperfections become very visible. By spraying very light thin coats, each coat was effectively too dry, and was creating a surface that was almost like very fine sandpaper. It is essential to create a completely wet surface for the paint to form a good finish. This needs some practice to get the feel of how much paint to put on in one go, because too much paint will flood detail, create sags and runs. However, you should not try to get a covering coat in one attempt. The colour will normally cover on the second coat.

Sometimes, if a large flat surface needs to be covered, in order to ensure that the surface is fully wet, you will need to deliver slightly more paint. To achieve this, move the needle back very slightly, by pinching it with your fingers adjacent to the locknut,

A little trick when a larger area needs to be covered: having loosened the nut that locks the needle in place, pinching the needle with my fingers adjacent to the nut will move the needle back slightly.

then retighten the lock nut. This will mean that paint will be emitted as soon as the air is released, and the trigger does not need to be pulled back to maximum.

AFTER SPRAYING

At the end of a spraying session, the cleaning process is started. It is very useful to have kitchen towel to hand for cleaning, and indeed throughout the model-making process. A normal sheet of kitchen towel is too big, so I fold it and cut it into several much smaller rectangles. This is a simple task to carry out

CONTINUOUS SPRAYING

When spraying a model, it is to be expected that a number of passes will be required to cover the model, as you move along its length or up or down its height. When I first learned to spray, I took the following approach: start to spray off the model, move across the model, stop spraying off the model, move down a little, start to spray off the model, move across the model in the opposite direction, and so on, until the model has been fully covered. This approach is still valid, with the exception that I no longer stop spraying after each pass. It takes time to stop then start again, and in this time the wet edge of cellulose paint will have started to dry.

Simple, soft and thoroughly absorbent, and just the right size to get inside small spaces when cleaning.

USING AN AIRBRUSH   31

between jobs, allowing the mind to take a break for a few minutes, or consider what is to be worked on next.

To clean the airbrush, first spray some neat cellulose thinners through. Before the thinners disappear completely, place some kitchen towel over the end of the nozzle, so that the air flows back into the cup, and bubbles appear in the thinners. This process is called back-flushing. With the TR2, it is the recommended way of cleaning the airbrush. With my other airbrushes, I prefer to dismantle the airbrush fully, to ensure every part is clean, particularly if I have been using a primer. Airbrush-cleaning brushes are available from Eileen's Emporium.

The mixing jars and stirrers must also be cleaned and then everything can be left to dry, before final reassembly.

Back-flushing, to clear blockages and also clean the paint out of the nozzle: with thinners in the cup and air flowing into the airbrush, seal the exit with a finger covered with a piece of kitchen towel. Allow the air to circulate the thinners around the nozzle and back into the cup.

The Paasche airbrush dismantles easily for cleaning.

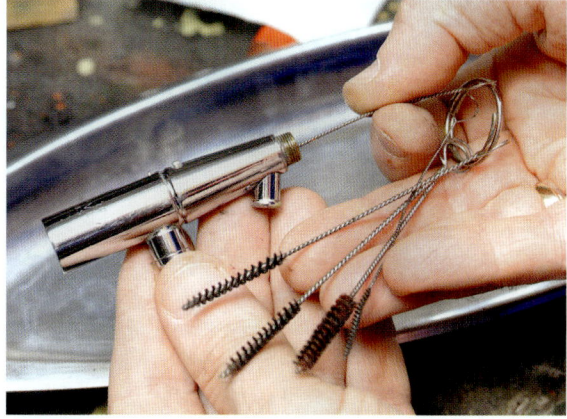

A very handy set of cleaning brushes for getting inside parts of the airbrush.

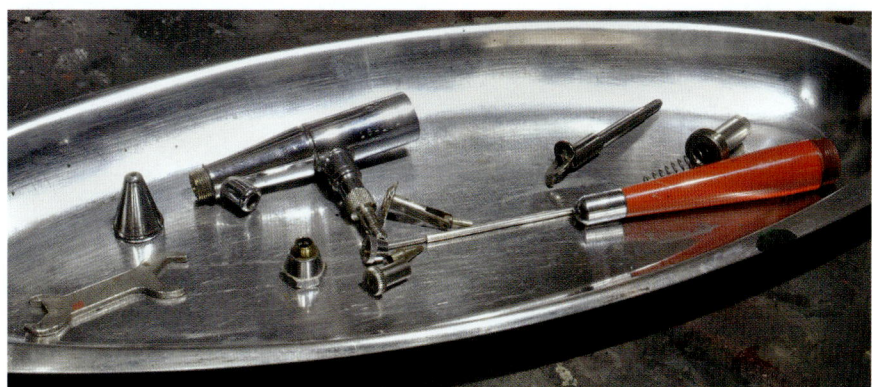

The Paasche fully dismantled during the cleaning process.

The Iwata can be dismantled somewhat further than this, but this is how far it needs to come apart for a general clean.

After each use, I always clean the mixing jars, which are actually the Paasche spraying jars.

CHAPTER FIVE

PAINTING

PAINT TYPES

The three main types of paint available for use when painting models are, in order of availability, enamel, acrylic and cellulose. There are a number of manufacturers producing enamel paints in authentic railway colours for model use and, in recent years, some manufacturers have produced railway colours in acrylics. There are a very limited number of specifically mixed railway colours available in cellulose, from one or two specialist model suppliers. There are a number of very extensive ranges of acrylic paints for weathering purposes, however (see later).

Enamel and acrylic paints are suitable for both spray-painting and brush-painting, however cellulose paints are really only suitable for spraying (although I have on occasion touched up minor damage to an area sprayed with cellulose paint with an old brush). Another important consideration to bear in mind when selecting paint types is which paints can be used on top of which paints, and also what surface is being painted. The issue here lies purely with cellulose paints. These can attack plastics, although they are safe to use on resin castings. They will also attack enamel paints that are already on a model's surface. The rule is, therefore, that cellulose paint must be sprayed on first.

This is a very small sample, some matt, some gloss, of the numerous and various enamel paints that I have in my collection.

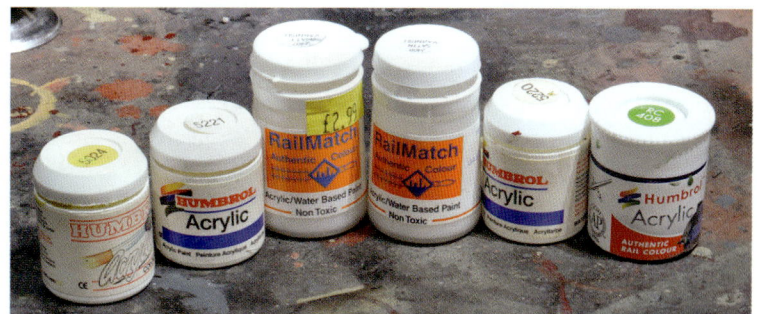

Acrylics often come in plastic containers.

The mainstay of my cellulose paints: green, black, red and primer.

WHY USE CELLULOSE PAINTS AT ALL?

If they are difficult to obtain and restricted in use, why bother using cellulose paints? There are benefits to this type of paint. It dries very quickly and, once it is on the model, this is a significant advantage. Whilst the paint is still wet, any dust that happens to be in the vicinity seems to be attracted to it, resulting in the need for rubbing down, and subsequent recoating, particularly if using enamel paint. Cellulose paints are generally touch-dry in a matter of a couple to a few minutes. Once the paint on the model is dry, another coat can be added. Cellulose paint can also be manipulated once it has dried. It can be rubbed down with a rubbing compound, then polished back to a gloss finish, without the need to recoat. This is handy if problems are encountered. Finally, the shelf life of cellulose paints tends to be significantly longer than that of enamels.

Cellulose paints are available from car-paint suppliers. The minimum quantity is normally half a litre, which for model use will last a long time, but will cost about the same as two 50ml tins of a railway colour in enamel. Hence, even if you choose not to use cellulose for the main body colour, it is still worth obtaining a tin of black in cellulose. It is important to remember, though, that the ratio of thinners to paint is probably the most critical when using cellulose paints. You will need in the region of three parts thinners to one part paint, in other words, significantly more thinners than with other paints.

Although I do not use aerosols for spraying, I do make use of the paint from them. It is a simple process to spray some of the contents into an airbrush jar, then add a small amount of cellulose thinners (between a quarter and a half of the amount of paint in the jar). It is difficult to be precise about the amount, but with practice you should develop a 'feel' for it – the paint should spray easily, but not be too thin.

Decanting paint from an aerosol can is a task to be done outside, and at arm's length. Squeeze the nozzle gently so that the paint is just coming out, and aim for the side of the jar.

Colours from the Halfords range that I use regularly.

PAINTING 35

The colours from a random selection of cans from a local car shop proved extremely useful; I am still using them over twelve years later.

Other types of thinners: with cellulose paints requiring a high amount of thinners, it is worth buying the larger can; anti-bloom thinners will help to prevent any dulling of the gloss; also seen are the thinners I use for spraying acrylic paints, and a thinner that comes as part of the Hobby Holidays weathering box of tricks.

Use simple white spirit from a major DIY store to thin enamel paint, as well as in the lining process.

MIXING PAINTS

Chiefly I use Halfords red primer, and matt black. Recently, I have painted a number of BR coaches and vans using Halfords Ford Burgundy Red, and in the past I have found Halfords Rover Henley Blue to be a close match for LNER Garter Blue. It is also possible to mix paints to achieve a particular colour. I have painted GWR coaching stock using a can of yellow, a

36 PAINTING

My home-made mixing spoons and stirrers.

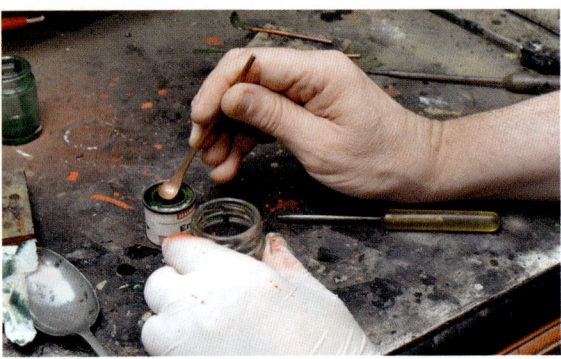

After a good stir, use the spoon to collect some paint from the tin, then take it to the jar.

With a pipette, measure some thinners, and mix into the paint in the jar.

can of beige and a can of brown that I found at a small local car-accessory shop. A 50:50 mix of the yellow and beige gave a very good representation of GWR Cream, and the brown with a small amount of black added matched a pot of GWR Chocolate. You can always refer back to enamel paints to check and compare the colours.

There are certain pieces of equipment that you will need for mixing paint. I have a handful of paint stirrers and measuring spoons that were made for me by my father from some copper rod. Other measuring spoons are available to buy, although I have not seen any that are angled like mine. I also have an old dessert spoon that I use for mixing larger quantities of paint.

Electric paint stirrers are available, but I have not used one of these since my school days. One reputable paint manufacturer recommended stirring paint with a bent paperclip mounted in a mini drill, set in a drill stand. With these items already in my tool kit, I thought I was well away. I put the drill on the slowest setting and carefully lowered it towards the tin. Seconds later, there was paint everywhere, including over my school shirt. (Of course, I had not bothered to change out of my school uniform when I got home.)

My paint stirrers seem to make a good job of getting into the sediment that sometimes sits at the bottom of a paint tin, and the measuring spoons are ideal for getting inside small tins to measure and transport paint to a mixing jar. I normally use one of the Paasche airbrush jars for this purpose. I have successfully mixed paint in the metal cup of the Paasche airbrush, putting the thinners in first – you can get away with this if the paint feed is from the bottom upwards, but with a side- or top-feed airbrush, the thinners will run into the airbrush. As a result, I always mix in a separate jar now.

PAINTING

If the model being painted is metal, it must be primed to help paint to adhere to the surface. When I first started painting models, I used a primer in a spray can from Halfords, but this is not the best way of achieving the necessary level of control to get into the corners effectively. Instead, I now use an etch primer, which can be sprayed through an airbrush. It is a 'two-pack' paint – in other words, the paint must be mixed with its activator prior to use. It must also be thinned with cellulose thinners to allow it to flow through the airbrush. The mixture of paint to activator to thinner can be 1:1:1 or 1:2:1. I have used both with equal success. More recently, I have found that this primer can be used on some plastics, as long as no cellulose thinners are added. In this situation, I have used the ratio 1:2 paint to activator.

After stirring, an old dessert spoon is used to measure the amount of paint, and then the amounts of activator and thinner.

The order of mixing is not important, but I generally start with the paint, then the activator, and finally the thinner.

My two-pack primer consists of the paint and a liquid activator. Once mixed, it should be used within an hour or two.

This is where my dessert spoon comes in handy. Give the paint a good stir with a large screwdriver, scraping the bottom of the tin to mix in the sediment. After a couple of minutes, transfer some paint to the spoon by dipping the screwdriver into the paint and letting it run off on to the spoon. About half a spoonful will suffice. Once the activator and thinner have been added, using the same spoon to measure the same amount, the jar of my priming airbrush will be three-quarters full. Give the mixture in the jar a stir with the small stirrer, then fit the lid and attach the jar to the airbrush.

THE SPRAYING PROCESS

GETTING STARTED

Your model has been cleaned, your compressor has been charged, and the primer has been mixed. Before spraying on the model, always test the spray on a separate sheet of metal. The purpose of this is to check that the airbrush is working properly and not blocked, with the paint flowing through properly, and that, when it lands on the surface, it gives the correct finish. This is also a chance to check that the paint mix is correct and to get the feel of the trigger position to deliver the amount of paint needed, and the spraying distance. If the test goes well, it is time to move to the model.

38 PAINTING

Try a test spray to ensure that the paint is flowing properly and that the paint is landing as you would expect.

The underside of the model is perhaps less important than the top side, so makes a good place to start.

Moving up the model, the steps and the cab interior are sprayed next.

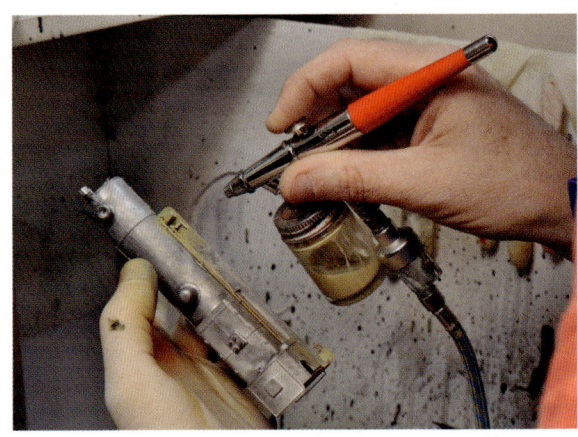

The next area to cover is the footplate and buffer beams, followed by the cab exterior.

Finally, the boiler is sprayed, varying the angle of the airbrush to ensure coverage behind the handrail. Finish on the area of the model that is most visible.

Start on the underside of the model – the parts of the model on which it will stand. Next, move to the underside of the footplate and boiler. With this approach, paint will also get to the underside of the valence and the underside of all steps. This will start to dry straightaway, and it will be safe to put the model down within just a few minutes. With the underside primed, start to move up the model. Spray the inside of the cab, and the footplate. Move on to the cab front, then round the smokebox, before finishing with the boiler and the cab sides and roof. Be careful to ensure that paint is getting into all of the corners and behind any obstructions.

PAINTING | 39

The tender is tackled in the same way: underside first, then interior, and finishing on the sides, the most visible part of the model.

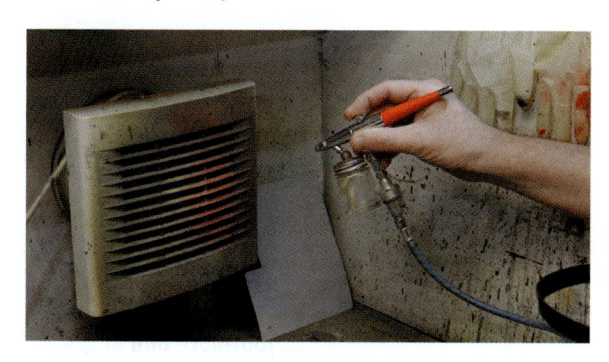

As soon as the spraying is finished, blow some thinners through the airbrush, then dismantle and clean. This is even more important after spraying etching primer.

Whilst cellulose dries very quickly, it needs time to harden. Enamel will take a matter of hours to dry, so a safe covered environment is needed. My propagator will go into the airing cupboard if necessary, to provide a warm drying area.

This can be achieved by varying the angle at which the airbrush is held to the model.

If you are using an etching primer such as this, the primer needs to coat the model, but does not have to cover it opaquely. However, there are times when it is advisable to apply more primer, such as on some white-metal surfaces, where the surface is not perfect. Such surfaces will need further work in terms of some light rubbing down and possibly some filling. Putting paint on to a model will highlight any imperfections in the surface, such as areas of unevenness or gaps to be filled.

Once the primer is dry, it is time for inspection. Check that the paint finish is smooth across the whole model, and check that there are no anomalies that require further work.

HOLDING THE MODEL

Some people are happy to put a model on to a 'Lazy Susan' (a turntable of the type often used in cake decoration) and then turn the stand for spraying, thereby avoiding having to hold the model. It is a personal choice. For me, it is just not comfortable. If I am holding the model, I have more flexibility to angle it to spray behind obstacles and into corners. I once had a gauge 2 LNWR Precursor to paint. It was very heavy to hold, so I tried placing it down to spray it, but it did not feel right at all. I ended up holding it in my left hand throughout the painting process – and significantly increased the size of my left bicep at the same time.

THE TOP COAT

After a wait of 24 hours, the next step is to apply the first body colour. If the loco is black, this is simple; otherwise, you will need to make a decision regarding the order in which you apply the colours. On the basis that I prefer to spray as much as possible, I will generally paint the black as the first colour. The alternative is to paint the main body colour, then add the black by brushing. However, in my experience this method takes just as long as masking the area does, and the black may well need a couple of coats before you achieve a satisfactory finish. Masking the main body colour to be able to spray the black tends to be too large a job. The principle is that, if there is masking to be done, you should do it over the smallest possible area. More importantly, if the black being used is cellulose, and the main body colour is enamel, then the black must be sprayed first, otherwise it will attack any overspray of the other colour.

Generally, black paint covers quite well, but it is wise to spray cautiously. Spray enough so that you can see that the surface is wet, but do not worry if full coverage does not occur at this point. Full coverage will normally occur with the second layer. If this does not happen, do not apply more paint in the same step; simply repeat as above. My normal order of spraying is to start on the underside and round the steps, then move on to the footplate, round the cab front, then the cab roof, then the smokebox, and aiming to finish with the cab sides and the boiler. Once this first coat starts to go off, another layer can be applied, again ensuring that the surface is fully wet.

PAINTING DIFFICULT AREAS

When there are obstacles, such as handrails, lubricators on the footplate, or other similar items of detail, additional care is required. If you focus on getting the paint behind the obstruction, the obstruction will generally receive a sufficient covering in the process.

One example of where the angle needs to be varied is on a tender underframe. Axle boxes are prominent castings, and need to be covered on all sides. My approach is to spray with the airbrush angled towards the underside, so that the bottom of the axle boxes is painted. I make several passes working up, allowing just enough paint to coat the area. This sequence of passes will paint the underside of the tender footplate as well. After it has had a couple of minutes to dry, move on to the sides of the axle boxes, angling the airbrush at 45 degrees to the tender frames. Target one side of the axle boxes

The black on the body of this model was brushed after spraying the green. After varnishing and light weathering, it is difficult to tell that it was not sprayed.

PAINTING 41

Hold the airbrush at an angle of about 45 degrees to the right. The aim of this is to cover the right-hand side of the axle boxes and springs.

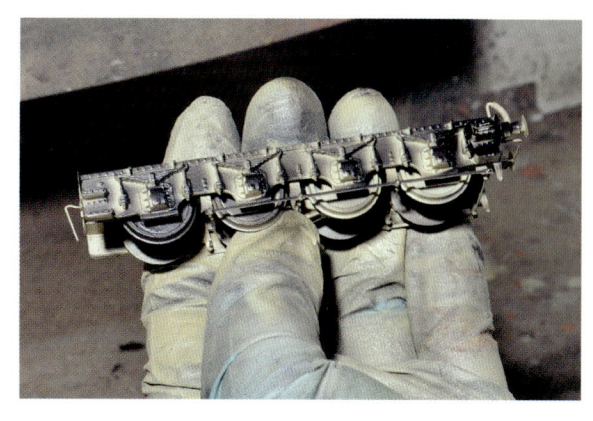

Check the results. One side of the castings should now be covered.

Repeat the process, aiming from the left at 45 degrees. Ensure the paint is getting right into every corner.

Check that both sides of the castings are covered.

The same process but aiming from above, to cover the top of the springs and axle boxes.

At this point, the only shadow of unpainted area should be that which will be covered when sprayed from below.

42 PAINTING

The penultimate pass, aiming from below to fill the last shadow areas.

The final light pass from the normal square-on angle, just to even everything up.

Finally, check that everything is covered.

at a time, then allow a couple of minutes before targeting the other side. Again, after another couple of minutes, take care of the tops of the axle boxes. Finally, another series of passes with the airbrush square on will even everything up.

Painting inside detailed cabs (where the firebox backhead is not removable) and behind smoke deflectors also needs consideration. These are difficult areas to access, but it is important to ensure paint coverage on them. It is better to get these areas out of the way early on in the spraying process. One reason for this is that it is easier to see how the paint has covered the concealed areas whilst the area outside is still light in colour, in other words, still in primer. This is one occasion when it is necessary to start the paint flow with the airbrush pointing at the model. To prevent any chance of paint spitting, check that the nozzle is clear, with no build-up of paint. This is far less likely to have occurred very early in the spraying process; it happens more often after spraying a lot of paint on larger areas.

Put the nozzle of the airbrush inside the cab, aiming towards the inside front of the roof in the corner. Gently squeeze the trigger until the paint just starts to flow, and pivot the airbrush so that the inside of the cab front gets a light covering. Paint down the vertical corners in the same way. The backhead itself does not present the same problem as the cab inside corners, and can be painted from slightly further back. Some models have a particularly large backhead; to get paint on the side of such a backhead, it is possible to spray through the window. Care is needed, as any stray paint on the way in will make a bit of a puddle on the outside of the cab.

PAINTING 43

If the cab furniture is fitted, then paint needs to get past this to land on the surface of the cab interior. Get the nozzle of the airbrush right inside, and spray a very small amount of paint.

To ensure that all areas inside the cab are covered, it may be necessary to spray through the cab windows too. Let the air flow, then pull back a little further on the trigger until the paint starts to flow.

Permanently fixed smoke deflectors also provide an obstacle to painting. Again, the airbrush needs to be close enough so that the paint just goes behind the deflector.

Apply paint from behind, in front and from above.

Aim the airbrush at the spokes of the wheel. With the air flowing, the wheel will start to spin, then you can squeeze a little more so the paint just starts to flow. The colour coverage will build up very quickly.

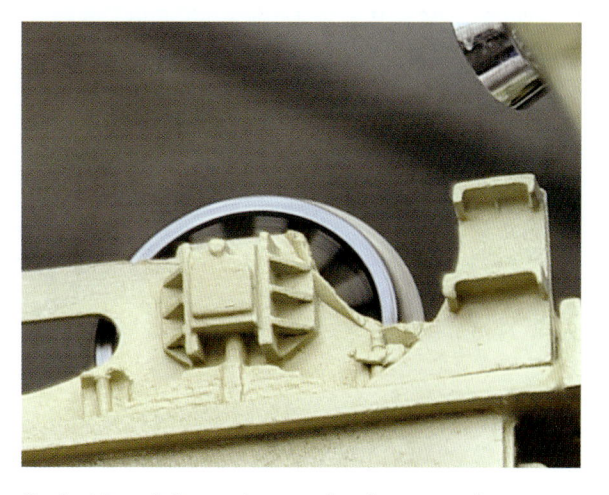

Both sides of the spokes need to be covered, so repeat the process from the other side.

44 PAINTING

Painting behind smoke deflectors requires a similar approach, applying paint from both the front and the rear.

Wheels require additional consideration. They will either still be on the model or they will have been removed. It is preferable to remove them (see later) for painting, but it is still possible to do the job where they are still fitted. The best way to apply paint evenly in this case is to have the wheels spinning. Position the airbrush at an angle to the wheel, so that the airflow will catch the spokes. Pull the trigger so that only air is emitted, causing the wheel to start spinning. Then pull the trigger slightly further so that the paint starts to flow. In seconds, the wheel will be painted on one side of the spokes. Angle the airbrush to hit the other side of the spokes and repeat.

MASKING

A window of at least 24 hours is now required, before you even consider applying masking to the model. If you have used enamel paint, it is advisable to wait at least two or three days, and possibly up to a week, to allow the paint to really harden.

There are a number of different masking tapes available, some for general use, available from DIY stores, and some specifically for modelling purposes from model suppliers. Tape used for masking must be strong enough to hold on to the area it is covering, but not so strong that it lifts some of the paint it is meant to be protecting when it is removed. The adhesiveness of the tape can be reduced a little by sticking it to another surface, such as a cutting mat, before applying it to the model. One added advantage is that the mat is a slightly more forgiving surface for the model being painted. Stick a length of masking tape to a cutting mat, and cut a piece of tape to the size you require. Some tapes are too wide for many situations, so it may be beneficial to cut the tape into strips of between 4 and 12mm wide. From this, cut lengths as required, peel the length off the mat, and put in place on the model.

Some standard masking tape lacks adhesiveness and can too often lift at the wrong moment, while red low-tack masking tape may leave a red residue when lifted. I tend to use either Frog tape, available from DIY stores, or Tamiya modeller's masking tape. There is little between them in terms of performance. In addition, I sometimes use a narrow tape from Tamiya that is useful for masking curved edges. Used in conjunction with the other masking tapes, it offers a degree of flexibility for difficult areas.

Masking products: the thin white tape can be applied to curves; the red tape is low-tack; the green tape is Frog tape; standard masking tape; and, finally, modeller's masking tape in the dispenser. Maskol is a liquid masking product.

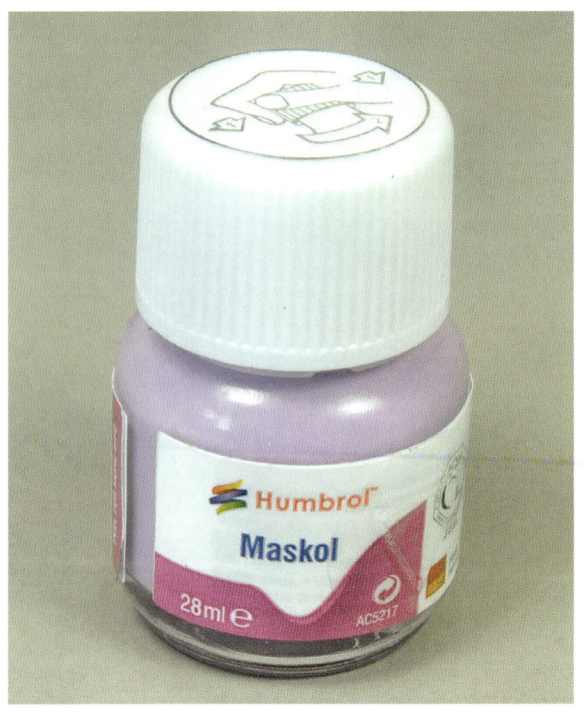

Maskol.

PAINTING 45

Applying maskol.

*ABOVE: **The black areas need to be masked, ready for the green to be sprayed.***

With a removable boiler, the masking job is rather simpler, as there is more space to gain access, even though there may be more masking to apply. However, masking this Castle was less time-consuming than the A1.

For larger areas, old newspaper can be stuck to the tape that is already on the model. However, it is important to ensure that these pieces are attached well, as, if they lift during the spraying process, stray paint will get where you do not want it. Also, beware of sharp areas, such as the ends of handrails, as these can cause tears in the paper, again resulting in stray paint.

One alternative, or perhaps supplement, to masking tape is Maskol. This is a liquid mask that can be applied to the model with a cocktail stick, and dries to a rubbery coating within a few minutes. It is not easy to be as precise as with tape for a sharp

PAINTING

straight edge, but Maskol is ideal on an area with a lot of detail, where it would be difficult or risky to apply tape.

After painting, ensure that all traces of the Maskol are removed as soon as possible. Use tweezers to pull off the majority, then a cocktail stick to rub off any small remnants.

Maskol should not be used if the next coat to be applied is cellulose. Cellulose paint sprayed over Maskol can react with it, making it virtually impossible to remove every trace. Also, whilst it is safe for up to a day or so, if it is left any longer it will

Start with the underside of the boiler and the footplate valence, then work upwards.

This tender body has been primed and the inside has been painted black. Now that it has been masked, a coat of red primer is being applied.

Focus on ensuring that paint is getting behind the handrail, rather than building up on it, by varying the angle of the airbrush.

Red can be a difficult colour with which to achieve coverage. The objective with the red primer is to provide a nice even base that will be easy to cover in one coat.

Ensure that the paint is getting into the corner where the dome meets the boiler. Allow the colour to build up with subsequent passes, until full coverage is achieved.

PAINTING

be difficult to remove fully. There are similar liquid masking products available, some of which may be suitable for masking prior to spraying with cellulose paint, but I have yet to try these.

With the black areas of the model now masked, the main body colour can be sprayed. At this stage, if the main colour is a red, I normally apply a coat of red primer, because red is a difficult colour with which to obtain coverage. A red undercoat is an ideal way of facilitating coverage of the top coat.

CHANGING COLOUR

Sometimes you will want to spray a second colour, perhaps on to another model, once you have finished with the first colour. You do not need to strip the airbrush down between colours (although, if I was spraying different types of paint from the same airbrush, I would try to paint cellulose first and enamel last, as cellulose is the easiest to clean, and enamel the most difficult). Spray through some cellulose thinners. I have some cheap ordinary cellulose thinners just for cleaning. Hold some kitchen towel over the end for a moment to backflush, then wipe out the cup. At this point, you can start to mix the next colour.

It is worth ensuring that at least the edge of the base has some top coat covering, so that no primer is visible once the model has been painted and reassembled.

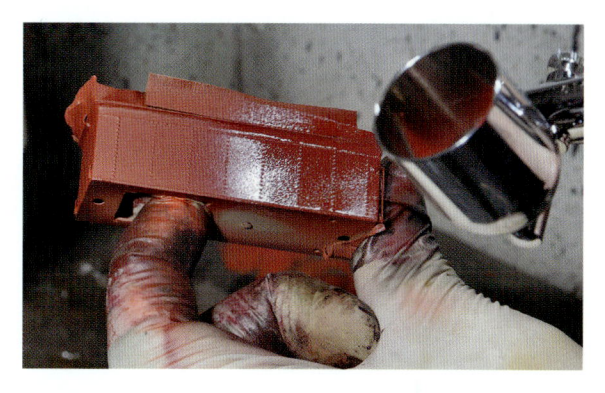

The initial passes deposit some paint, and coverage is achieved quite quickly with the red undercoat. This is an enamel paint, in Midland red.

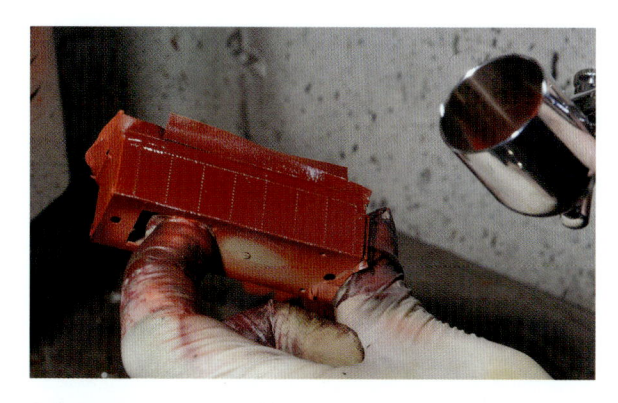

Subsequent passes will put enough paint on to achieve the wet surface that is required for a good finish. Too much paint will result in sags, as enamel takes hours rather than minutes to dry.

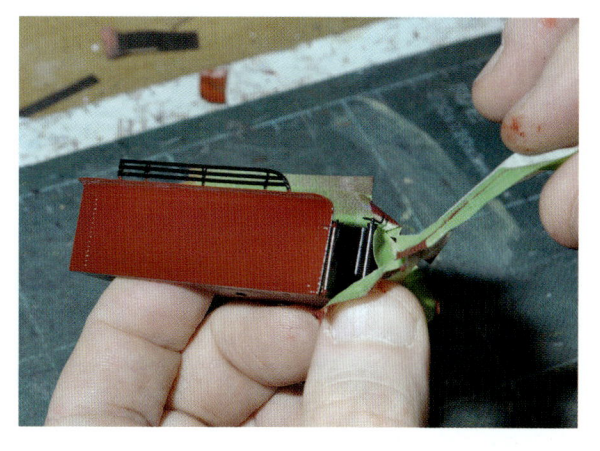

At last, the reveal stage: the model takes another step towards coming to life.

PAINTING

The M&SWJR 2-6-0 after having the red sprayed. I had a change of heart on the cab and footplate assembly. The black had been sprayed, but then I decided it would be easier to spray the red, then mask the red to spray the black. This is the reason for the overspray on to some of the black areas.

The main colour coat can be applied in the same manner as black in terms of building up the colour. Start with the cab sides and front, then move on to the boiler. The final passes will be enough to wet as much of the model as possible.

Sometimes, items can be sprayed with a second colour without masking. It is largely down to being able to spray the item at an angle that protects the already painted surface. Some tenders, particularly if they have an outward flare at

The M&SWJR 4-4-4 with the Midland red coat added. Just the buffer beam red and the lining to go.

One of the sandboxes from the M&SWJR 2-6-0. The top is black and the sides are Midland red.

By holding the airbrush at an angle of about 45 to 60 degrees to the bottom of the sandbox, the sides can be sprayed without masking the top.

the top, can be treated in this way. The inside of the tender can be sprayed, then the outside can be sprayed, keeping it tilted to protect the inside. Another example of this that I came across recently was a pair of sandboxes, part of a Midland and South Western Junction Railway 2-6-0.

As soon as the spraying is finished, the masking should be removed, with great care. Enamel paint will still be wet, and cellulose and acrylic paint will not have gone off fully. Masking must be removed before the paint dries, to prevent a hard edge forming. Also, if there has been any overspray on to part of the model that was meant to be masked, it must be removed before it has dried and hardened. If the overspray is cellulose, it can be removed with some T cut (as used on cars, and available from car-accessory stockists). A small amount of T cut applied with a cotton bud or similar will polish off the unwanted paint. The T cut can then be washed off in water, ensuring that there is no powder left on the model. If the overspray is enamel, it can be removed with a brush and some white spirit. Wet the brush with some white spirit, dab the brush on some kitchen towel so as not to soak the area (otherwise some paint pigments may float off into difficult-to-access corners), then carefully soak up the unwanted paint, and dry the brush on the kitchen towel. You will see the colour of the paint soak into the towel. Repeat this process until all the unwanted paint is removed.

Sometimes, but thankfully not that often, the masking tape will pull off some paint as it is removed from the model. This can be because the masking tape was just a bit too sticky, or it could be just plain bad luck. Once you have finished cursing, you need to look at how to rectify it. The worst-case scenario is that the whole model will need to be stripped and the whole process started again. However, this is not always the case. If the area is easy to access, then perhaps just that panel will be affected. Generally, this will involve going back to bare metal for that panel. If some paint has lifted, there will be at least a slight edge, a step down to the surface below the paint that has lifted. This could be the primer, or it could be right back to the bare metal. If you attempt to spray over this, the step will still be visible.

The whole panel – for example, up to some kind of edge or corner, or a boiler band – will need to be rubbed back with wet and dry paper, or fibreglass pencil, getting back to the bare metal. Once it has been cleaned, masking needs to be reapplied around the area.

There are some exceptions, however, if the area where the paint has lifted is less critical, and perhaps is due to have a degree of weathering applied. In that situation, touching in with a brush should be enough to sort out the problem.

PAINTING WHEELS

Wheels that cannot be removed easily from the model can be painted in situ, but my preference is to remove them if possible. If they can be removed from the axle, they can simply be mounted on to card with some double-sided tape. If the wheels cannot easily be removed from the axle, as with a locomotive driving wheel set, where you do not want to have to re-quarter the wheels, or perhaps some tender wheels that simply drop out as a set,

The simplest way of spraying wheels. Remember to vary the angle of the airbrush to ensure that both sides of the spokes and the inside of the rim get coated, rather than just the facing edges.

PAINTING

When a wheel set needs painting, cut a pair of slots into some card that has been bent around and put the axles into the slots. Here, the bearings of tender wheels are being masked by the card; this approach can also be used for a pair of driving wheels with the motor and gearbox in between.

MASKING WHEELS

Clearly, the tyre treads, flanges and the backs of the flanges need to be free from paint. Whilst the back of the wheels is generally protected from paint by the card, inevitably the tyre tread and flange will get a coating of paint unless it is masked.

I have tried masking this part of the wheel in the past, but found it to be a little fiddly. As a result, I generally now spray the wheels without masking, leaving me with a cleaning job after the painting process. This is simple enough with a scraper and a fibreglass brush, and in my experience takes no longer than the job of masking this surface would have done.

then the whole wheel set can be mounted on to some card with cut-outs for the axles. This way, the card will mask the bearings on the axle.

BRUSH-PAINTING

As much as I prefer to spray, there are times when only the brush will do. Sometimes it is just impractical to mask, due to space or lack of access. Examples include detail items on the top of side tanks, axle boxes and steps where the background colour is different.

I always like to ensure firebox backheads are painted, and this needs to be done with quite a fine brush. Reference to photos is ideal for this.

I have tried to brush-paint buffer beams on various

The toolbox on this tank was not practical to mask when spraying.

When dealing with tender frames that are not black, I would paint the axle boxes and the frames (including any lining) before fitting the axle boxes. However, if they are fitted, they will need to be brush-painted after the main colour has been sprayed.

PAINTING | 51

The steps on this tender are black, so they need to be brushed in.

The backhead of the ex-MR Big Bertha. As it is one casting, it is that much more important to distinguish the various pipes and gauges.

The backhead in this Castle has a number of separate castings, but it is still worth picking out the detail with paint.

The interior of a 7mm GWR steam railmotor. The seats were painted before fitting. They were first sprayed black, then the pattern was achieved by holding some mesh out of an old tea strainer over the cushion, then spraying with white.

PAINTING

With the surrounding area masked, a coat of red primer is first added to the buffer beam.

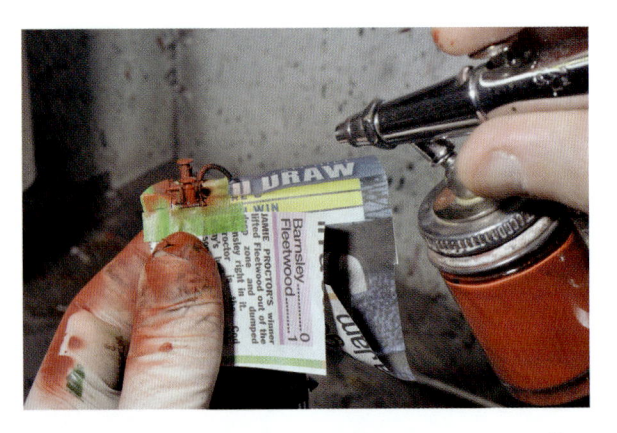

The buffer beam has a lot to spray, in a very small area, so all angles of approach need to be utilized.

If possible, couplings should be added after painting, having been painted separately. On this model, the coupling will be brush-painted after the buffer beam has dried.

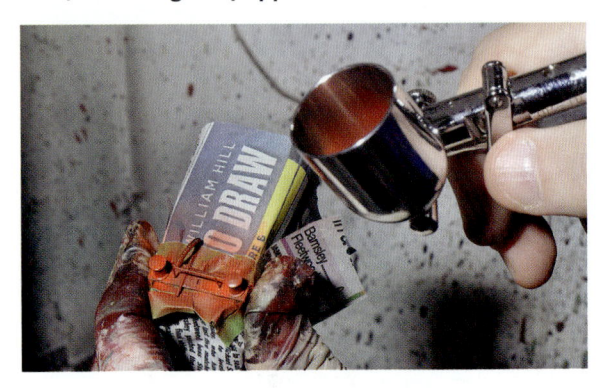

Once the red primer undercoat has been sprayed, in the time that it takes to clean the airbrush and mix the red top coat, the buffer beam will be ready to take the final colour.

The buffer heads will need to be brushed black or Gunmetal, once the red has dried. If sprung buffers are used, then the buffer heads would be fitted after painting.

occasions, with a variety of paints from different manufacturers, but I have never been happy with the result. It has always proven difficult to get coverage without numerous coats, and it seems to be impossible to avoid leaving brush marks. Although I am in a minority in this respect, my preference is to spray buffer beams. This does mean that time needs to be spent in masking around the beams, but in my view this is offset by the time taken to brush-paint and recoat.

Once the buffer beams have been masked, start by spraying a coat of red primer. I use a spray can of red oxide primer, sprayed directly into the airbrush jar, and thinned slightly with cellulose thinners. It does not take long to dry, so it is safe to apply the top coat shortly after the primer. For this I use an enamel.

PAINTING | 53

Again, the big reveal, as soon as possible after painting, so the paint is still wet.

Pull the masking tape off slowly, to minimize the risk of removing any of the paint underneath it.

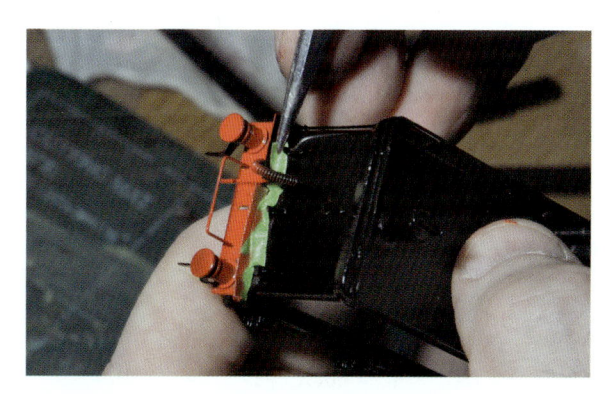

The various small pieces of tape used to do the masking. Whilst I would use as big a piece as necessary, it is easier to feed smaller pieces behind and between small items of detail.

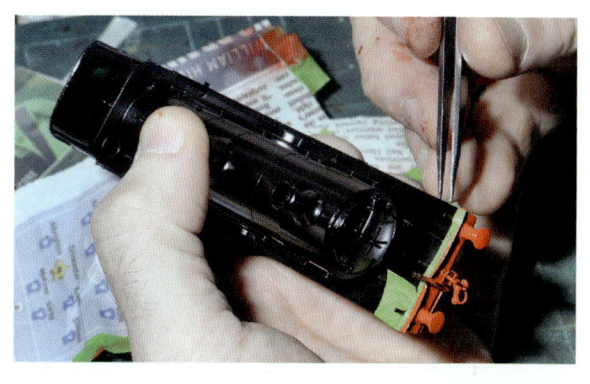

A thin piece of tape in front of the lamp irons and a wider piece behind, then another piece would have been over the lamp irons. Despite the low pressure of the air through the airbrush, paint will find any gaps in the masking.

The couplings, buffer heads and vacuum pipes are ready to be brush-painted. Finally, I will scrape the paint of the shaft of the buffer behind the head with a craft knife.

Another pair of buffer beams ready for finishing. As this model has sprung buffers, the heads will be added next, prior to weathering.

USING FILLERS

Recently, a number of models built from cast white-metal kits have come to me for painting. They have been built to a high standard, but some of their surfaces have been less than consistent, which is a common issue with white-metal castings. As a result, I have had to apply some filler to a number of examples recently. In theory, the best time to apply the filler is before the painting process; however, sometimes it is the application of primer that helps to highlight where the filler is needed. There have also been occasions when the need for filler only really became apparent once the top coat had been applied.

I use a cellulose putty, sometimes called knifing putty, which is available from car-accessory shops. It comes in a tube and can be applied straight to the model without mixing. Push it well into the area that needs filling, and scrape off the excess, then leave to dry. Within a few hours, the area can be rubbed down with some fine wet and dry paper. Clean the area with water to ensure that all remnants of the rubbing down have been removed, then, once dry, painting can continue.

Halfords knifing stopper is an ideal filler. It does not require any mixing and dries quickly, ready for rubbing down.

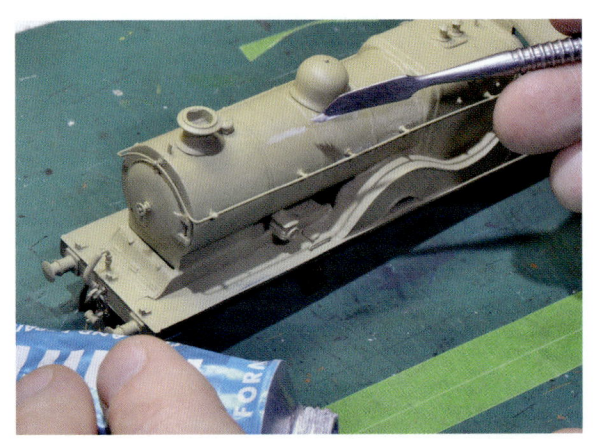

The filler is easily applied using a flat tool. Another area requiring filling on this D9 is visible just above the handrail in front of the firebox.

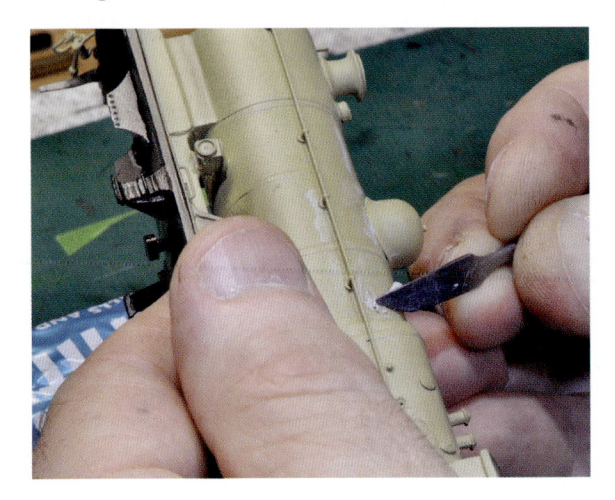

Apply the filler by pushing it into the area that needs to be filled, then scrape across the surface to remove the majority of the excess.

When the recess has been filled, and most of the excess has been scraped off, leave it for about an hour to harden before rubbing down.

PAINTING | 55

Sometimes, the need for filling only really becomes apparent once the top coat is on.

As before, the filler is applied and most of the excess removed.

Once hardened, the filler is rubbed down with 600-grit wet and dry paper until smooth.

water. The surface was then washed in water and, once dry, more coats were applied. In the end, I think I performed the rubbing-down process three times on this model.

This A1 has been filled and smoothed and now awaits further painting.

Another example of a model that needed extra work was an LNWR Precursor, built in gauge 2. An old model that needed a lot of cleaning, it was spoilt by a number of construction marks, such as filing scraps in the surface. There were too many for me to take care of them all, so I focused on the tank and bunker sides, which is where most of the marks were and where imperfections tend to be most visible. I filled the majority of the marks, then applied a number of coats of paint. This was achieved by spraying, letting it dry for a few minutes, then spraying again, and repeating a few times. Then, once the paint was fully dry, the surface was rubbed down with 600-grit wet and dry paper dipped in

The surrounding area is masked – the footplate, the smokebox, and the rest of the boiler from the third boiler band.

56 PAINTING

Whilst the newly re-sprayed area looks glossier than the other green areas, this will be evened up when the model is varnished, after lining and numbering.

The porous nature of the castings of this very old model meant that the tender sides did not look right.

Some rubbing down and recoating achieved a far smoother finish.

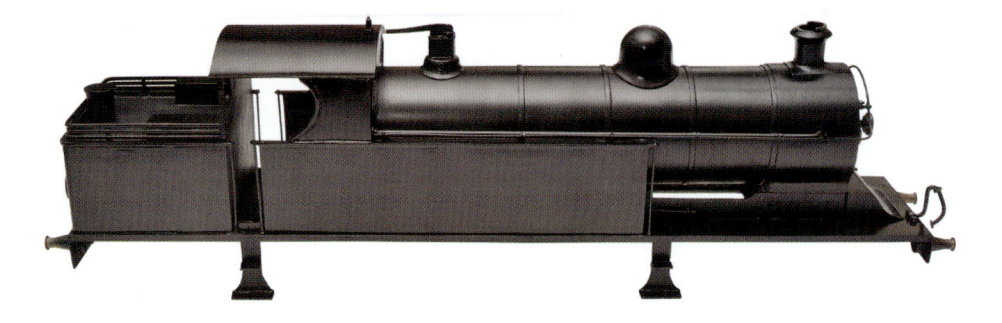

After a significant amount of filling, rubbing down and recoating, the tank and bunker sides have a completely smooth finish.

PAINTING 57

Much of the surface of this model was not great, but the eye is drawn to the vertical flat areas, so getting these right will greatly improve the appearance of the finished model.

COMPOSITE MATERIALS

EARLY GWR COACHES

Sometimes, a model that has been made from both metal and plastic will require painting. In this case, priming of the metal surface is essential for paint adherence, but particular care is needed when priming plastic. I have subsequently found that my two pack-primer is safe to use on some plastics, providing no cellulose thinners is used in the mix, but I had not ascertained this when three four-wheeled GWR coaches came to me for painting. The roof of each coach was plastic, as were the sides of one of them. The plastic areas were masked prior to priming, then I sprayed a small amount of primer on to the gas lamps on the roof, before spraying the interior. It is advisable to spray the interior before the exterior, as the frames of the windows up to the glazing should be the same colour as the exterior. Once the interior has been sprayed and has dried fully, masking tape can be placed over the windows from the inside. In this way, when the main body colour is applied, the sides of the window frames will be taken care of.

The underframe provided some additional challenges in getting a coat of paint to cover all areas. The main issue was covering the gas cylinders, without over-painting the steps. The approach is to concentrate on getting the paint on to the cylinder, whilst keeping an eye on the steps to ensure that the paint is not building up. Have the airbrush close and squeeze the trigger so that only a small amount of paint is sprayed. During this process, you will normally find that the steps are effectively covered sufficiently, and will not need a further pass of the airbrush.

These GWR coaches have brass ends, and one has plastic sides, but both have a plastic roof.

PAINTING

With the plastic areas on the GWR coaches masked, priming can begin.

Once the metal areas have been primed, the main colours can be sprayed.

I prefer to spray the interior colour first, then mask the inside of the windows, so that the inside of the window frames will be the same colour as the outer body colour.

PAINTING 59

I painted the roof next, then masked to paint the ends, but the main aim is to finish with the sides, as these are the most prominent.

The underframes of the GWR coaches were all metal, and removable from the bodies, so were simply primed then sprayed with matt black.

Careful spraying was needed to cover the gas cylinders without overloading the steps.

3D PRINTED GNR G1

Another recent job that came to me was a GNR G1. The main superstructure of this model had been 3D-printed, along with brass fittings for the handrails, whistle, buffers, lamp irons, coal rails, and so on. I have seen some models that have been 3D-printed before and have been a little sceptical about various aspects, in particular the finish of the surface. This technology is in its infancy for the hobby of model-making, but it is certain to be significantly refined over time.

This particular model had had most of its surface smoothed to a degree. I prepared it with just a water wash, as the detail parts had been glued on rather than soldered, then a light brush over with white spirit to ensure it was fully degreased. It was initially primed with my usual primer, but with a mix of one part paint, two parts activator, and no cellulose thinners, in case this had a reaction with the plastic. As soon as there was some paint on the model, any imperfections were highlighted. There were some areas that needed further rubbing down, and some areas of the surface had microscopic holes. At this point, I came across a different primer, which was acrylic and is also described as a micro filler. After a test off the model, then on the underside of the model, I applied a coat to the outside. Once fully dried, the tank and bunker sides were rubbed down with 1200-grit wet and dry, and, after cleaning under the tap, another coat of the acrylic primer was applied. This

The body of the G1 was produced by 3D printing, so a lot of rubbing down was needed before and during the painting process. FRANK BULKAN

A 4mm scale GNR G1 that came to me for painting and lining.
FRANK BULKAN

RIGHT: **This product was recommended for this particular project. It sprayed perfectly through the airbrush straight from the bottle without any thinning.**

PAINTING | 61

process needed to be repeated and the model then required about three coats of the acrylic primer before it was smooth enough for the top coat.

With the model being predominantly plastic, I only used enamels for the main colours. With this in mind, I could take a different approach to the order of applying the body colours, as the issue of cellulose paint before enamel was not relevant. I decided to do the smallest areas first, as this would simplify the masking process. The buffer beams were sprayed red first, followed by the valence, which was sprayed in Great Northern Red-Brown. With these areas masked, the black areas were then sprayed, and then all but the areas to be sprayed green were masked prior to the final colour being added.

PAINTING TEAK

Painting a teak-effect finish on to a coach makes for an interesting and satisfying project. This is a two-stage process. First, a light beige/yellow base coat needs to be sprayed evenly over the body. I have used different colours on occasions, but Humbrol 63 is a good place to start. Then, when this has fully dried (at least 24–48 hours later), the top coat can be added. This must be thinly brushed, effectively creating streaks representing the grain, which is the base coat showing through. The direction of the brush strokes is important, so that the 'grain' is in the correct direction. This tends to be parallel to the longer side of the panel, so will be vertical for the higher panels, and horizontal for some of the lower panels. The colour can be varied very slightly between the panels by using a couple of shades of brown that are mixed in a palette, and by varying the amount of each colour.

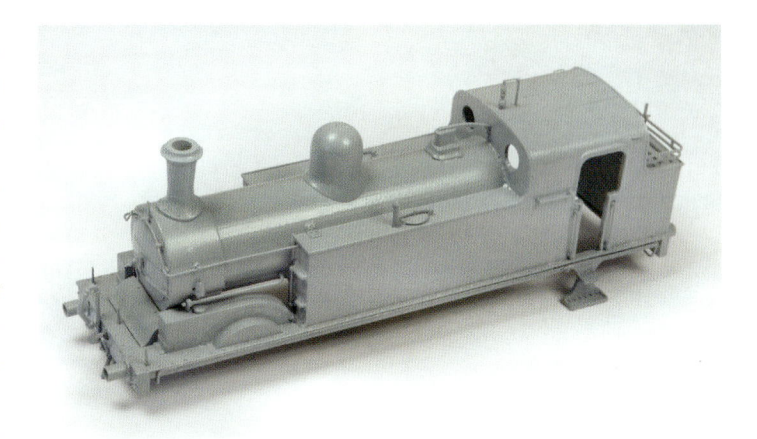

I primed the G1 model with my normal primer first to ensure that all the metal areas were suitably prepared, then a number of coats of the Microfiller primer were applied, rubbing down between coats.

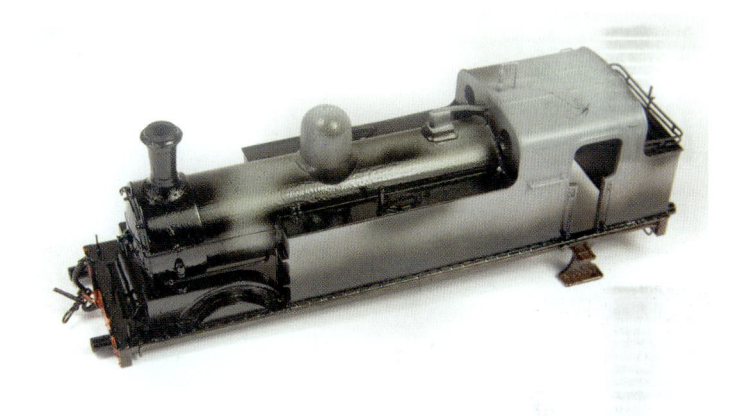

Once primed, the buffer beams were painted, followed by the valence and steps in GNR Dark Red, then the black. Painting the smallest areas first reduced the amount of masking, as each colour was sprayed.

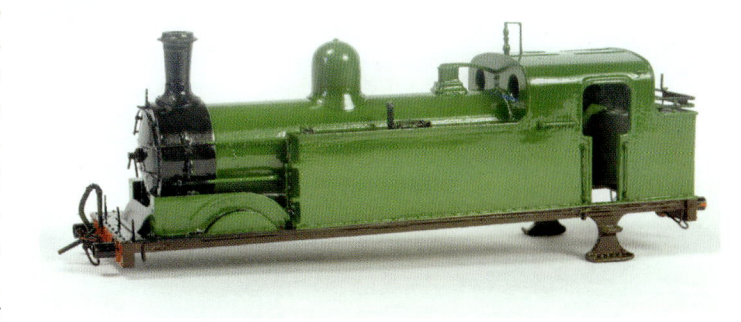

Finally, all other colours were masked on the G1, and the main body colour of Doncaster Green was sprayed.

62 PAINTING

These ex-Great Northern Railway coaches were built from etched brass kits in 4mm scale and have removable underframes and roofs. The teak colour really brings them to life.

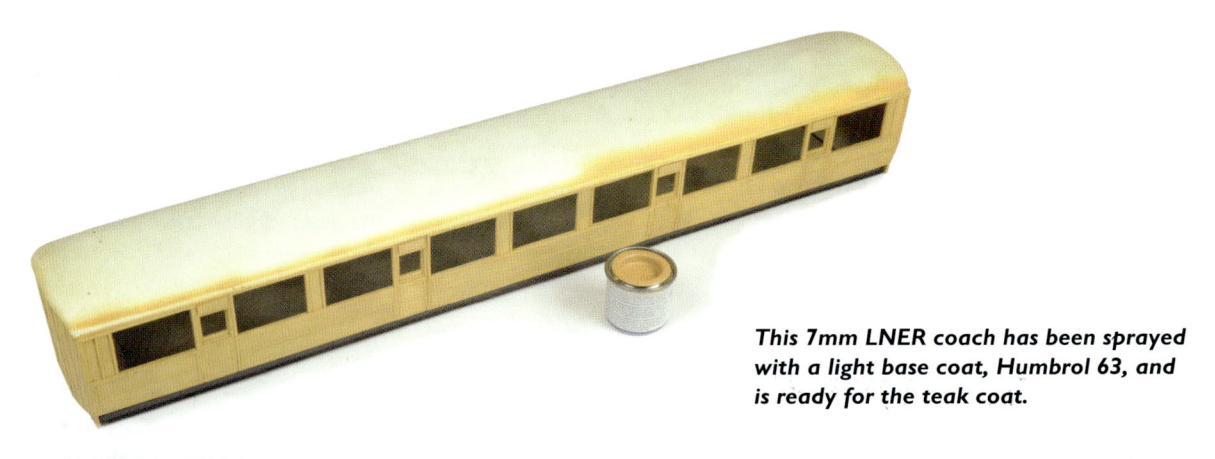

This 7mm LNER coach has been sprayed with a light base coat, Humbrol 63, and is ready for the teak coat.

ABOVE LEFT: A selection of brown paints is used to obtain the teak grained effect.

ABOVE RIGHT: With two or three suitable browns in a paint palette, and a brush that is not one of your front-line best, draw in a small amount of each paint and stir with the bristles.

LEFT: As you draw the brush along the panel, you will see the teak effect forming. Be careful to note the direction of the grain of the wood on the panel you are painting; some ran vertically and others were horizontal.

PAINTING

Once the teak effect had dried on the 4mm coaches, red lining was applied to the raised beading. Once that was dry, a slightly thinner yellow line was added.

It is particularly important to make close reference to photographs of the prototype when doing this. Ideally, you should have a photograph the size of the model and put this next to the model as you paint it. This is another aspect that is worth practising before painting the model.

ALTERNATIVE APPROACHES

In order to illustrate that other methods do work, I would like to take a look at a rake of kit-built O gauge ex-LMS coaches that I bought a few years ago, when I found I was not getting the time to build some of the kits I had. These were built and painted by Brian Flanagan, who described to me how he had approached the painting.

Each coach has the roof glued to the body, which in turn is bolted to the underframe. The coach body and the underframe were painted separately. Both were first given a coat of Halfords grey primer, straight from the can. The underframes then had a coat of Halfords Satin Black, followed by a coat of dirty black, made by mixing three parts Humbrol Satin Black, two parts Humbrol no. 29 Dark Earth and one part no. 70 Brick Red, allowing at least one day between each colour.

After grey primer on the body, the inside of the roof was sprayed with white primer. This was then masked and became the final colour for the inside of the roof. Then, the outside was sprayed using an airbrush with Phoenix Precision gloss BR Cream.

My rake of ex-LMS coaches, built and painted by Brian Flanagan in the early British Railways livery of Carmine and Cream.

PAINTING

This livery has been applied with an aerosol primer, followed by airbrushed enamels for the main colours.

This construction has a permanently fixed roof and a removable underframe that reveals the separately painted interior.

The lining is a commercially available transfer and the varnish is from Railmatch. In a ratio of 4:1 satin:gloss, it gives a very satisfying sheen.

Two days at least after this, the yellow was masked with Tamiya tape and Phoenix Precision gloss BR Crimson was sprayed on to the sides. Getting it to cover, particularly round the doorways can be hard, and usually three or four passes with the airbrush are required. After at least another two days of drying time, the coach body was masked and the roof painted in Humbrol no. 67 Dark Tank Grey. The next day, the ends were hand-painted with Humbrol Satin Black or the mix of dirty black. It usually takes two coats. The interior was painted Humbrol 63 Brown.

Lining was added in the form of transfers, together with the numbers and emblem. Door handles and grab handles were added at this point and, finally, the sides were varnished with Railmatch satin varnish and gloss varnish in the ratio of 1:4.

PAINT STRIPPERS

At some point, paint is going to have to be removed. It could be that a problem is encountered at some point in the painting process, or perhaps a model is acquired that needs to be repainted in a different livery. In certain circumstances, it may be possible to paint a new livery over the existing livery, otherwise the model needs all the paint to be stripped.

I have used three different strippers, although other strippers are available. Perhaps the best-known is Nitromors, which is the most extreme

PAINTING | 65

Various strippers (left to right): model-specific stripper; a general stripper that is safe on plastics and glue; and Nitromors, for really stubborn paint. (Nitromors will attack plastic, glued areas or skin.)

that I have used. It has a strong odour, it will burn your skin if you get it on you, and it will attack plastic and glue. There are a number of anecdotes that recall someone putting this chemical on to a model, leaving it for a while, and returning to find it reduced to a pile of components, as the model had been glued together. I now use Nitromors only occasionally, and then only on metal that has been soldered, where the paint is particularly stubborn.

At the other end of the scale is the Phoenix Precision paint remover. This is a fairly thin liquid and can be reused if the paint removed is filtered. I have done this in the past, although I have not been particularly successful in regaining significant amounts of the stripper after this process.

The stripper that I make most use of comes from one of the DIY chains. It is far safer than Nitromors and more economical than the Precision option. As with the other strippers, it is applied with a brush, left for a while to work, then the surface is given a good scrub, before being washed off with plenty of water.

Stripping paint ranks high on the list of my least favourite tasks. Whichever stripper I use, small stubborn patches of paint remain, which then need to be removed with scratch brushes or other scrapers. In fact, the whole surface of the model benefits from a clean with the scratch brush, and then all the fibreglass debris needs to be removed. Areas of fine detail are particularly vulnerable during this process and great care needs to be taken.

Whichever stripper is used, some paint is always left after the first strip. Apply some more and leave it to work before washing and scrubbing off.

Eventually, any remnants of paint will need to be attacked with the fibreglass brushes.

CHAPTER SIX

BOW PENS AND OTHER LINING PENS

TYPES OF PEN

The most commonly used tool for lining is a bow pen, otherwise known as a ruling pen. This is an old draughtman's tool and does not particularly resemble a conventional pen. It has traditionally been used with inks, but can also be used with paint. The width of line that is drawn is governed by the distance between the jaws, which is controlled by an adjustment screw. These pens can be found through various sources online, such as eBay. Manufacturers of top-of-the-range bow pens include Kern and Haff. All bow pens will easily take paint, but only the better pens will be able to produce narrow lines consistently, without requiring some work first. Some bow pens have the facility for one of the jaws to pivot, which considerably facilitates the cleaning process; this can then be carried out without disrupting the line-width setting.

Some curved lines follow the curve of part of the model, such as a splasher or a footplate valence, or the curve of a tender panel. Some

The front line of my lining tool kit: a normal bow pen, a small bow pen attached to a pair of compasses, and some very fine brushes.

The pivoting jaw is a very useful facility, as the jaw can be swung open for cleaning, then clicked back into position, without changing the width setting. The line on the dial gives an indication of how far the dial is turned when adjusting the line width. Only small adjustments are needed.

My two Winsor and Newton Series 7 brushes, size 000 and 00, have been well looked after. They were expensive, but they are still giving excellent service, despite being several years old. According to one top model painter, with these brushes you will surprise yourself with what you can paint.

BOW PENS AND OTHER LINING PENS

liveries call for the side of a wheel to be lined. In each of these scenarios, a bow pen fitted to a pair of compasses can prove very useful. When applying the lining to the edge of a wheel, the compasses are used in the normal way to draw a circle. For the more complex shapes, the compass point can follow the profile of the line, for example by following the edge of the footplate valence.

Cheaper bow pens can make excellent lining tools, after some re-shaping on a sharpening stone. My main pen cost me less than £5 from a stationer's shop about 30 years ago. It has a pivoting jaw, which is particularly useful for cleaning, as it can be cleaned without changing the line-width setting. After some careful grinding work to the end of the jaws, it has consistently produced numerous high-quality narrow lines.

Some bow pens have numbers on the dial of the adjusting screw. This is a useful facility, but not essential, and neither of my pens has it. Instead, I engraved a straight line across the dial, to indicate how much I am turning the dial when adjusting the width of the line. It facilitates very small adjustments.

The Bob Moore lining pen, with two tracing attachments.

For the areas where bow pens cannot reach, and for the tight corners of panels, high-quality brushes are needed. I use specific brushes for this purpose and keep these brushes just for this use. I was recommended to use Winsor and Newton Series 7 brushes, size 00 and 000.

Also in use, although less common these days, are Rotring pens, or similar, which are much more like a conventional pen. They are designed to take ink, but there are some paints available specifically for these pens. The width of the line is controlled by the size of the nib, so a small selection of sizes would be required. Such pens are simple to use, handling in a similar way to a conventional pen. However, although I have had a degree of success with them in years gone by, I just use a bow pen for lining now.

There is also the Bob Moore lining pen, which takes enamel paint. I do not have one of these in my own tool kit, but I have managed to borrow one to try out. These pens tend to be more commonly used in the larger scales. The width of the line is governed by the head, so different widths are obtained by changing to different heads. These pens can be used against a ruler, or an attachment to the head will allow an edge on the model to be followed.

My old collection of Rotring (and similar) pens, and the paint they use. On the far right is the cleaning fluid.

OTHER TOOLS REQUIRED FOR LINING

Lining models involves very fine work, which needs to be viewed very closely. In recent years, I have started wearing glasses for reading and model-making, but some years ago I bought a magnifying visor. I did not use it a great deal at the time, as I did not do that much lining then, but it is now invaluable in the process, and also when checking that lettering and numbers are level when applying transfers. I did wonder whether using such a visual aid would have an adverse effect on my eyesight generally, but I was reassured by my optician that it would not be detrimental. However, I prefer not to use it for long periods.

I use the magnifier simultaneously with my reading glasses. It comes with four different lenses and a small LED light, although the light is not particularly effective.

The other tool required in the lining process is a pair of dividers. These are needed for marking out where lining needs to be positioned on the model, and also for measuring and marking where corners need to be painted in. In order to make a very small scratch in the paint, which will be covered by the resultant line, one of the points on the dividers needs to be quite sharp. Grinding one side slightly more pointed than the other will allow you to make a small mark without any pressure.

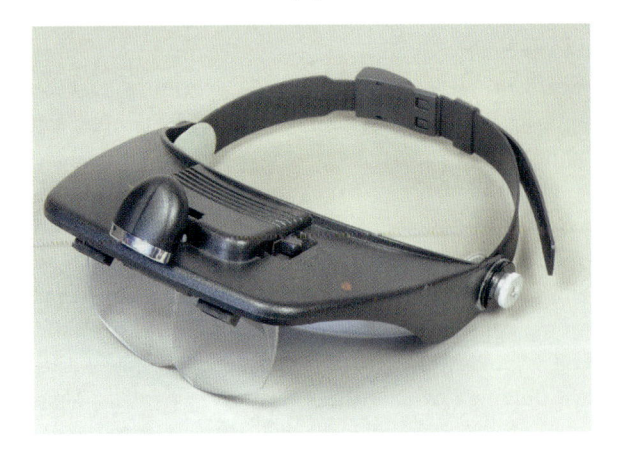

These dividers are used for marking on the painted surface of models where the lines need to be placed; they can then be painted with the bow pen.

Grinding one point of the dividers sharper than the other will allow you to make a precise mark on the paint surface with the minimum of pressure.

My magnifying visor has become essential in giving me a close-up view of lining.

USING A ROTRING-TYPE PEN

Lining with Rotring-type pens is similar to lining with a bow pen, but slightly easier, because the Rotring pen behaves and handles in a very similar way to a conventional pen. Paint is added to the reservoir with the pipette that is in the top of the paint bottle. Positioning the pen on the model adjacent to the steel rule to paint a line is simple as it is easy to see exactly where the pen will paint the line. This process takes a little more getting used to with a bow pen.

Over time, despite being cleaned with a specific cleaner, the pens became blocked and stopped working. It was at this point that I started practising with bow pens for lining.

BOW PENS AND OTHER LINING PENS 69

The paint used in Rotring pens is water-based, and comes complete with a pipette in the lid for easy filling.

Bearing in mind this is a 4mm scale model, Rotring pens are very effective lining tools.

Completed many years ago, this LNWR milk van and full brake was lined with Rotring pens.

This LMS auto coach was completed at about the same time as the LNWR model, again with Rotring pens.

The auto coach stands up to fairly close scrutiny.

BOW PENS AND OTHER LINING PENS

USING A BOB MOORE LINING PEN

This pen comes with an instruction sheet, two attachments to facilitate tracing an edge, and a drill to clear the tube if paint is allowed to dry in it. I tried it with some paint that I know flows well from the bow pen. A few drops of paint are put into the top, which is then drawn down the tube by capillary action, and the pen is ready for use. The instructions suggest the use of lighter fuel to help the paint to flow, but I do not keep that in stock and I did not find it necessary. Once the paint had flowed down the tube and had come into contact with the metal surface, it flowed freely. I also tried one of the attachments for tracing an edge, which worked well.

For me, the drawback was that there was only one head, which was a little on the large size for 4mm and 7mm. Smaller heads are available, but I like the ability to adjust the width of a line with the simple turn of a screw. Also, there were two tracing adaptors, but they are for tracing at a fixed distance only. However, with a little practice, high-quality lines are very possible with this tool.

The tracing attachment fits on to the painting head.

The tracing attachment allows the line being drawn to follow a parallel edge.

My first attempt at painting lines with the Bob Moore lining pen.

USING A BOW PEN

Ruling pens, more commonly known now as bow pens, can be very versatile tools for painting high-quality and very narrow lines. However, they can take some getting used to. Demonstrating lining at a model exhibition not long ago, I got talking to someone about the use of a bow pen. I offered him a try with my pen. I put some paint in, painted a couple of lines on my test piece to adjust the pen to a nice narrow setting, and made sure the paint was flowing, then I passed him the pen, rule and test piece. He put the pen to the metal surface and moved it along. Nothing came out. After a couple of attempts, I helped him to adjust the position of the pen, and the angle to the surface, then the paint started to flow and, after a few more attempts, he started to produce some decent lines.

This encounter reminded me of when I first picked up a bow pen. It was a while before I managed to get

BOW PENS AND OTHER LINING PENS

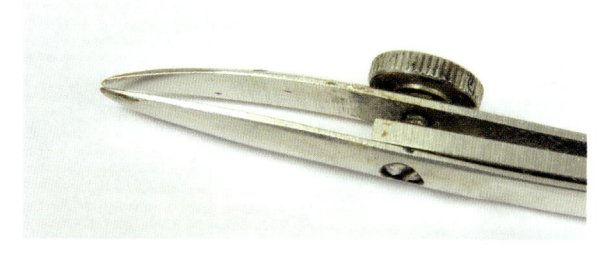

Close-up of my main bow pen, showing the shape of the jaws and the way in which the inside meets the tip.

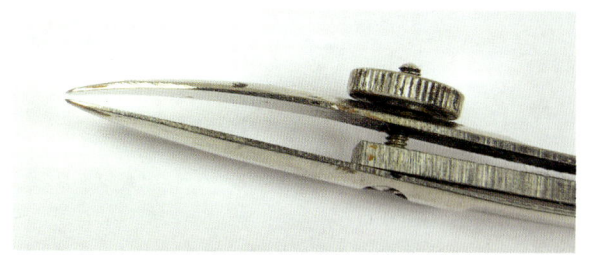

From a slightly different angle, some of the grinding marks are still visible and it is clearer how the jaws come to a point.

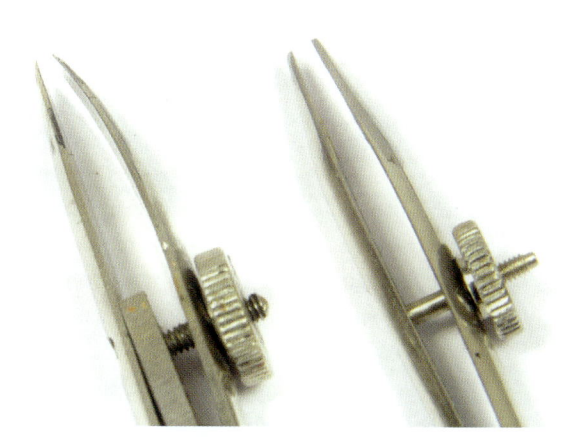

My pen on the left, next to a pen that needs some attention to the tips of the jaws.

The lines on the top of the sheet were painted with my bow pen. The next set of lines was painted with the other bow pen before any work on the tips.

the paint to flow. Even now, when I go through my scrap plasticard box, I come across a piece that has many thin lines painted on it, the result of practising with a bow pen. However, with practice and with a pen with decent jaws, they are simple and effective tools for painting lines.

Set the bow pen jaws to almost closed – in other words, with a very small gap at the end. Having stirred the tin, pick up enough paint on a cocktail stick so that it will drop off after a couple of seconds. In that couple of seconds, move the stick to the pen and allow just one drop to go in between the bow

PAINT THICKNESS FOR BOW PENS

The paint must not be too thick, nor too thin. If it is too thick, it will not flow, and if it is too thin, it will run out of the sides of the jaws. If the paint is slightly too thin, then it will appear weak, and the colour will not be as strong in appearance as it should be. Unlike when spraying, slightly thicker is better than slightly thinner. Generally, the consistency of a newly opened tin is ideal. I do sometimes add some thinners to the paint before loading it into the pen, but that is normally after I have tried the paint and found that it is not flowing well enough to produce sufficiently thin lines.

72 BOW PENS AND OTHER LINING PENS

Just one drop from the cocktail stick is enough for plenty of lines. Two drops will be too much.

Put the pen up against the ruler and draw it along slowly.

The angle of the pen is almost upright, tilted only very slightly inwards. My test sheet is used every time the pen is filled.

pen jaws. This should be enough for double lines around both sides of a tender at least. More often than not, the paint will start to dry in the pen and cease flowing as freely before it runs out.

Move to your paint surface. I always try the pen on a test piece before moving to the model, after every refill, just to check all is well and to get the paint flowing properly. Place the rule on the surface, then bring the pen into contact. No pressure is needed. Your hand is simply holding the pen and guiding it. Judging the distance between the edge of the rule and where the line is painted is a matter of practice and experience, but it is a little further away from the edge of the rule than it is with a Rotring or Moore lining pen. Slowly draw the pen along the edge. The actual speed is difficult to describe and so much easier to gauge when you see it. It needs to be slow enough to be able to see the consistency of the line being drawn, but not so slow as to result in a jerky movement.

PREPARING A BOW PEN

There are certain techniques that can be used to improve a lower-quality pen. You will need a sharpening stone and an eye glass, to be able to look very closely at the tips of the pen.

The tips need to be almost sharp and the inside face must reach straight down to the tip. To this end, the outside of the pen must be honed to remove excess metal and the treatment applied to each jaw must be exactly the same. Examination with an eye glass will help to check on this. The grinding process involves rotating the pen almost 180 degrees with each stroke along the sharpening stone, to remove the metal right around the tip of the pen. Keep checking as you go along, working on both jaws, then, with the jaws open, see if they will cut through some paper fairly easily.

Now, the tips need to be blunted slightly. If the tips are left sharp, they will mark the surface as the pen is drawn across it whilst painting. Keep the pen perpendicular to the sharpening stone in a north–south

BOW PENS AND OTHER LINING PENS

To grind the tips of the bow pen, place one jaw on the sharpening stone, in the position shown.

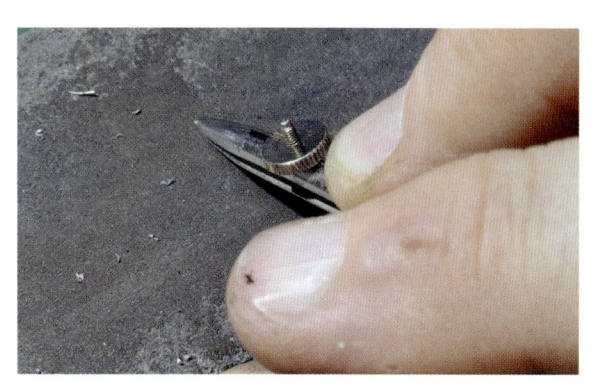

Draw the pen along the stone, rotating the pen as it moves.

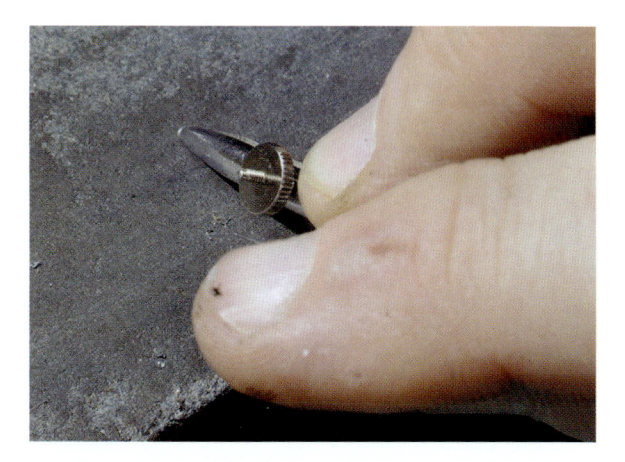

When the pen has been rotated almost 180 degrees, stop and repeat the process.

Keep checking how the tips are looking with an eyeglass.

direction (as held, so that both jaws are in contact with the stone at the same time throughout), but at an acute angle in the east–west direction, leaning towards the direction in which you will move. With a rotating motion, draw the tips along the stone until the pen is now at an acute angle in the east–west direction and leaning away from the direction of motion. Only a few strokes are needed to take the sharp edges off, then, after some cleaning, the pen is ready for testing with some paint.

The angle of the pen is quite critical to the outcome, but there are a few degrees of latitude. Generally, the pen should be almost at right-angles to the surface, although I tend to have it leaning slightly towards myself. Sometimes, when I am

Once both jaws have had the same treatment, try cutting some paper with the tips.

BOW PENS AND OTHER LINING PENS

Place the tips on the sharpening stone, ensuring both tips remain in contact with the stone throughout the stroke.

Again, rotate the pen. Only two or three passes are necessary.

The new profile of the tips after grinding.

BOW PENS AND OTHER LINING PENS | 75

putting a third line between two existing lines, I have changed the angle very slightly to move the position of the line a little.

One high-quality bow pen brought to me had had some extra honing done to the tips, before being sold at an exhibition as ready for use. For some reason, I could not get the pen to perform at all. I took a close look at the tips. They had been honed to different lengths; if I held it at an angle of perhaps no more than 60 degrees to the horizontal (tilted significantly towards myself), then good-quality lines could be painted.

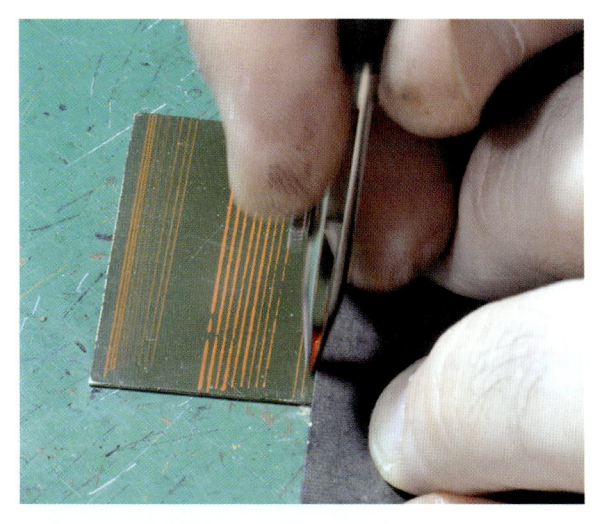

When testing, do not judge the performance on the first couple of passes; allow the paint to get flowing.

Look to see that the lines are even, and that the tips are not marking the surface of the paint. If they are, they are still too sharp.

After a few more lines I am happy with the result.

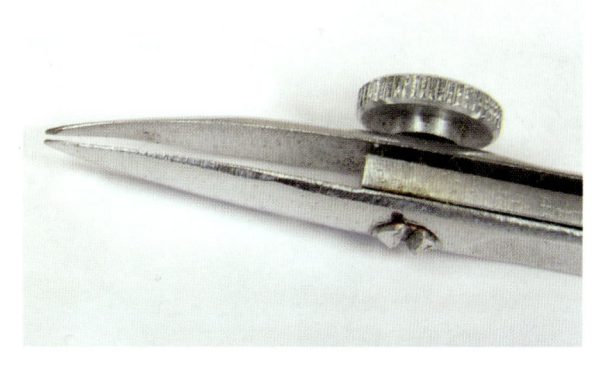

A pen bought on eBay for just a few pounds. The ends need cleaning up somewhat and the jaws do not meet perfectly, so a grinding job will be needed in order to create a decent tool.

CHAPTER SEVEN

LINING

STYLES AND OPTIONS

There are a number of different types of lining. Starting with locomotives, there are generally two styles: border lining and inset lining. LMS red livery incorporates border lining, where the lining is applied around the edge of panels. LMS black livery and BR liveries include inset lining. This is where the lining may follow the shape of the panel, but is inset from the edge.

This means there is an extra step when dealing with the model, in deciding exactly where the lining needs to be.

The next consideration is whether there is more than one single line. Are the colours adjacent to each other, such as the cream and grey of BR black and LNWR liveries, and the black and white of LNER and Southern liveries, or is there a gap between the lines, where the main body colour would be visible, such as GWR and BR green, between the orange and the black? If there is a gap between the lines, then each line is a single line that must be correct and clean. When lines are adjacent, whichever colour is subsequently applied, then this line can be used to edit the previous line by thinning it.

With regard to coaches, the obvious question is whether the coach is beaded or flush-sided. A flush-sided coach again presents the issue of locating the lining correctly, although this is simpler than on a locomotive, as the lining can generally be positioned in relation to the windows. With a beaded coach, generally the lining will be applied on to this. However, for some liveries the lining is actually applied to the edge (effectively the side) of the beading. This is possible on the model, particularly in 7mm scale, although this does depend on the quality of the beading. For example, on coaches that have been built from an etched brass kit, the beading corners can be rather inconsistent, and in places fade away to nothing. Whilst it is possible to

The ornate express passenger livery of the LMS involved border lining on its locomotives. However, this border consists of four separate lines, red–gold–red–black.

This 7mm LNER J83 is based on the Edinburgh Waverley station pilot – another example of border lining.

LINING

An example of inset lining: British Railway's final express passenger livery was a slightly simplified version of the GWR express passenger livery.

Another example of BR inset lining. We will look at the curved line at the front a little later.

The LNER mixed traffic livery had inset red lining.

Whilst the loco has border lining, the tender has a combination of both, with an inset panel on each side.

The red line on this proprietary model should be less than half of the width of the grey line and there should be a thin cream line adjacent to the inside of the grey line.

This model has been lined with commercially available transfers; again, the two lines appear to have the same width.

On this hand-lined model, the relative widths of the lines are much more accurate, as is the gap between the lines. Also just visible is the very thin cream line on the inside of the grey line.

achieve a good result, it was impossible to line the side of the beading; instead, the lining has to be put on to the top (in other words, the surface that faces outwards from the model).

The next consideration is the method for applying the lining. The main methods are commercially available lining transfers, Rotring-type pens, and bow pens. I have used all three methods, but I just use a bow pen these days.

Finally, there is the question of which colour to apply first. The general rule is to deal with the most prominent colour first, as this is the most important to get right. However, there are exceptions to this. If a line is particularly narrow, and touches another colour, then it is possible to thin the first line with the second line. Examples of this is the cream line of LNWR/BR black lining, which is an eighth of an inch wide. This is 0.04mm in 4mm scale and 0.07mm in 7mm scale. Also, the most ornate form of LMS red livery lining incorporates red–gold–red–black, each of which adjoin each other. The red lines are again so narrow that it is advisable to thin them with the adjacent colour. However, care is needed, as the second line can be affected by the first line, as the pen rides over the edge of the first surface

As an example, with GWR/BR green livery, the orange line would be painted first, being the most visible. The first time I attempted this livery, I could not believe the width of the orange lines – an eighth of an inch – even having measured it on a 12 inch to the foot locomotive. They are so prominent. It is next to impossible to produce a line this narrow with even the best lining pen, so it is advisable to use a less prominent colour instead of orange. A suitable and commonly used substitute is Humbrol 9, Gloss Tan.

TRANSFERS

'Transfer lining' means using commercially available lining transfers, as opposed to transfers that I have made myself. For more on this, see later, 'Boiler Bands'.

An example of commercially available transfer lining that I bought for a model a number of years ago, in case my hand-lining was not up to the task.

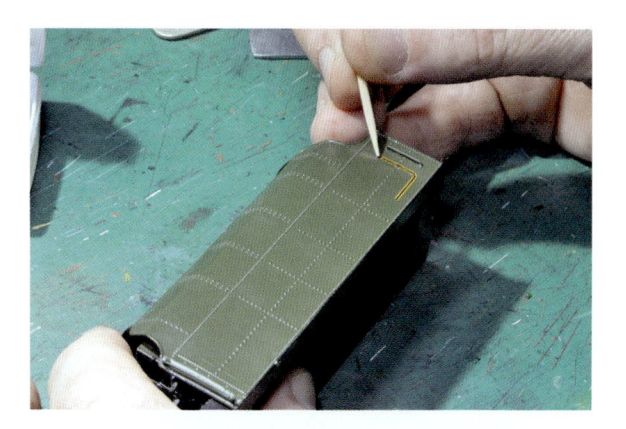

When applying a lining transfer, start with a corner, ensuring that the line is both horizontal and vertical. Whilst it is still wet, the transfer can be moved with a cocktail stick.

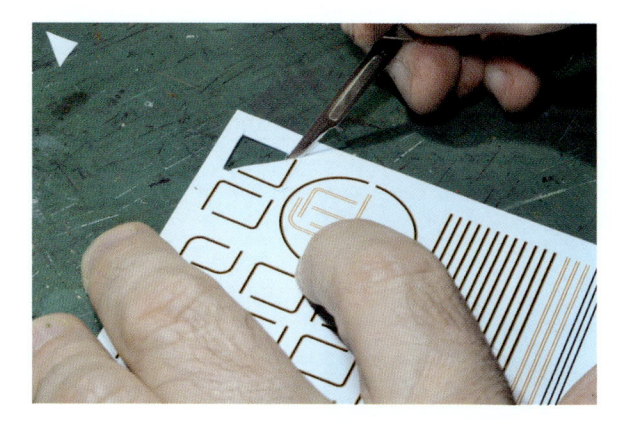

When cutting out the corner pieces, it helps to cut them out as a triangle, as this will keep the lines at right-angles as long as possible.

After soaking in water for a few seconds, take the transfer still on the backing paper to the model, and slide it on to the model.

Connect the two corner pieces with a long straight section. This is best done before both the corner pieces have set, in case some adjustment is required. If any of the transfers need to be loosened to move them, apply some Micro Set.

Work up to the next corner.

It is not uncommon for the curves provided on the sheet to fail to match exactly the curves you need on the model. Select the closest match, then make a series of cuts in the transfer to allow it to be manoeuvred into a more suitable radius.

The finished tender side. This lining should have very thin (eighth of an inch) orange lines, then a green gap either side of the 1-inch black line, but this is not the case with this transfer.

A3 60039 Sandwich lined with transfers.

LINING | 81

Lining transfers are generally waterslide transfers, which are cut out, soaked in water and then slid off the backing paper on to the model. Straight lines are not normally a problem, as the transfers just need to be cut to length. There may, however, be an issue with curves. Whilst the sheet of transfers will have some different radius curves, it may not have exactly the curve you need for your particular model. In this case, the closest match will need to be adapted by cutting and flexing into position.

From normal viewing distances, the transfer lining is perfectly adequate.

A3 60103 Flying Scotsman lined with transfers.

With simple rectangle panels and identical right-angled curves at the end of each line, this model is ideally suited to transfer lining.

82 LINING

Another example of a transfer-lined model.

This K3 has a variety of different curves on both the cab sides and the footplate valence. With patience, a good result can be achieved with commercial lining transfers.

LINING COACHES

BEADED COACHES

Generally, the lining on coaches is a little more straightforward, as the lines tend to be straight, and on flat surfaces, which are for the most part easier to get to than some areas of a locomotive. There is the exception of some pre-grouping liveries, where clerestory roof panels and underframes were lined. However, there tends to be more lines on coaches than locomotives, which will mean, once started, there is plenty of opportunity for practice.

An example of a model that is simple to start on yet can produce quite an ornate livery is the Midland Railway clerestory coach. In 4mm scale, Ratio, Branchlines and Slaters produce kits of various examples of this type of coach. One added benefit of these coaches is that the panelling has square rather than curved corners. This makes the model an excellent opportunity to practise positioning straight lines.

The lining can be applied directly on to the beading, starting with the gold. Except for the beading around the edge of the coach, the gold needs to be applied to both edges of the beading. The width of the gold is not critical at this point, as the black line is applied adjacent to the gold, and can be used to trim the gold. Start with the horizontal lines before the vertical lines, as it is easier to avoid the former with the ruler, whilst applying the latter. I find it easier to apply the line to the lower edge of the beading. Line the rule up level with the bottom of the beading and paint the line. Work along the coach in one direction, applying the line to one side of each bead, before turning the model round to do the other side of the beading.

After at least 24 hours have elapsed, the black lines can be added. Take the same approach as with the gold, horizontal then vertical, lining the ruler up with the gold line. Again, work along one side, then turn it round to do the other. If necessary, additional black lines can be added adjacent to the first to fill the gap, or it can be brushed in between the lines.

LINING 83

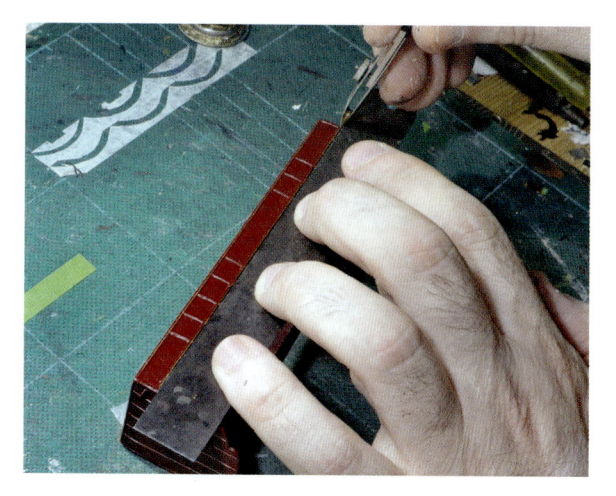

The gold lines being painted on to a 4mm scale Midland Railway coach. Starting with the horizontal lines, I will put a gold line on both edges of the beading.

With the horizontal lines in place, the vertical lines can be added. Unless the horizontal lines have had 24 hours to dry, take care not to touch them with the ruler.

Work along the coach putting the line on one edge, then turn the coach around and put the line on the opposite edge.

The black line needs to be completely central between the two gold lines. Whilst lining up the ruler, I will make a test mark at the end of the line to check the position first.

A similar mark is then made at the start of the line.

Once the ruler is in the correct place, the line can be painted.

84 LINING

The vertical lines are done next, in the same way.

Move the bow pen at a fairly slow speed (you will have found the optimum speed whilst practising on your test piece), but focus on trying to keep it as constant as you can.

The beaded panel behind the door handle needs to be black, with a black line either side. It can be filled in with repeated lines with the bow pen or with a brush.

Using a French curve, find a suitable match for the curve of the tumblehome on the end of the coach side, then paint the line.

Review progress as you proceed. With almost every line being straight, and with a beading to show where the lines need to go and right-angled corners, this model is an ideal starting point for lining practice.

LINING

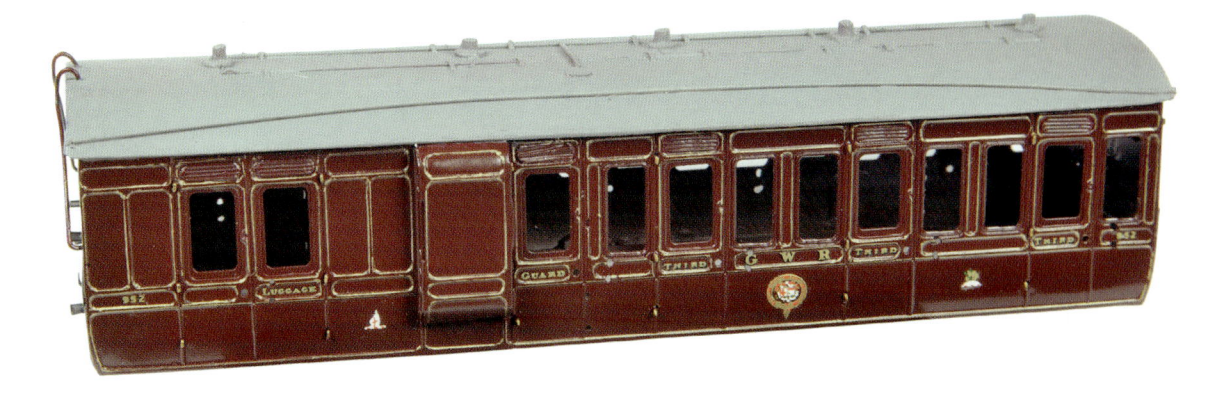

A 4mm scale coach in the early GWR crimson livery. There is a gold line around either side of the beading, following the curves. The curves were brushed in after the straight lines had been painted with the bow pen.

A sister coach to the 4mm scale coach in early GWR crimson livery. The lining has actually been positioned on the side of the beading, rather than squarely on top.
JOHN DANIELS

The Midland and South Western Junction Railway livery was very similar to that of the Midland Railway, but slightly simpler, with black ends, no lining below the body, and yellow rather than gold lines. PHILIP HALL

86 LINING

The second and third of three M&SWJR 4mm coaches. These are beaded, but the etchings were not great and the beading was a little inconsistent in some places, so I had to paint the lines where the beading was meant to be. Door handles and grab handles were added after painting and lining, and after varnishing, so as not to leave a shadow that did not receive the varnish. PHILIP HALL

FLUSH-SIDED COACHES

A number of years ago, I started an Airfix LMS non-corridor coach with a pair of Comet sides fitted, painting it and then putting it away for a long time awaiting completion. It is useful to demonstrate the pseudo panel lining of yellow and black that was initially applied to flush-sided coaches.

The principle is the same as with beaded coaches. If there are any lines that are not around the edge, or not adjacent to a window, then indicate where they need to go with a light mark in the paint with a pair of dividers. Again, paint the horizontal lines first. By painting the lines adjacent to the windows first, the subsequent lines will be easier to position. Place the rule over the windows, level with either the top or the bottom of the window, then paint in the line. Then turn the model round so that you can see the freshly painted line, whilst you paint in the second yellow line. Apply the vertical lines in the same way, starting adjacent to the windows.

Once the straight lines have been applied, paint in the curved corners of the panels. If neces-

The lines on this flush-sided coach for this livery are above, below or adjacent to windows. The horizontal yellow lines were painted first, then the vertical lines. They were all painted on one side of the windows first, then the model was turned around to paint the lines on the other side of the window.

Known as 'pseudo panelling', the panels on this livery have curved corners that need to be brushed in.

LINING 87

It may be easier to paint from the inside of the curve, so work first from one side, then turn the model round to do the curves that go the opposite way.

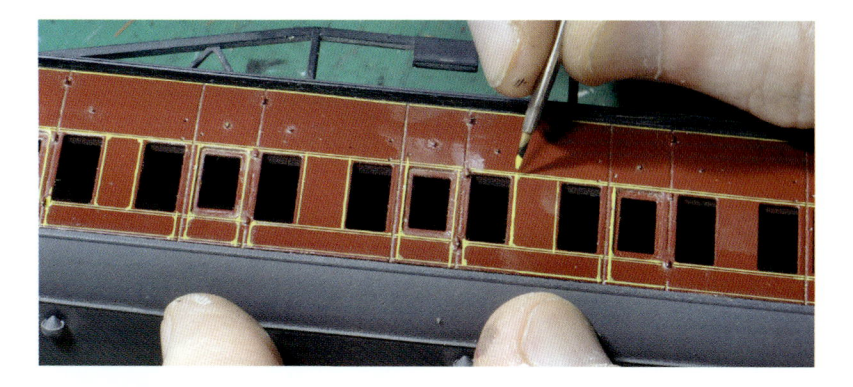

If necessary, tidy the curves with a clean brush moistened with white spirit then blotted on kitchen towel, so that only a very small amount of white spirit remains on the brush.

This coach, which started out as an old 4mm scale Airfix coach and then had replacement Comet sides put on, was painted a few years ago. It really could do with a re-paint of the main body colour, but it usefully illustrates the lining of a flush-sided coach.

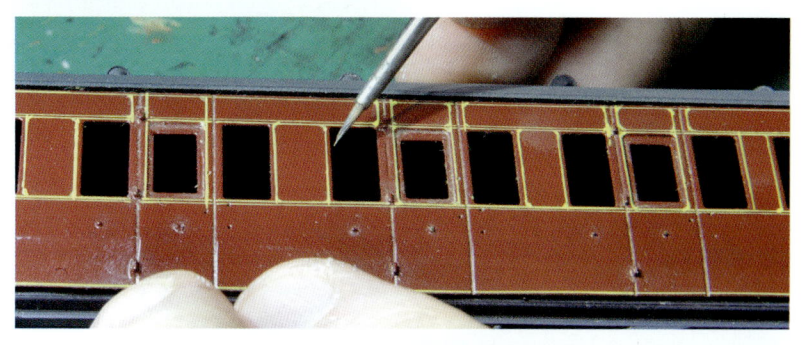

sary, they can then be tidied with a brush and some white spirit.

Again, wait at least 24 hours before applying the black, in the same way as with the beaded coaches, then brush in the black curves at the corner of the panels.

Once the yellow is dry, the black can be added. The bottom line is painted first, then the waist line, both with the body upside down, giving me the best surface for my ruler.

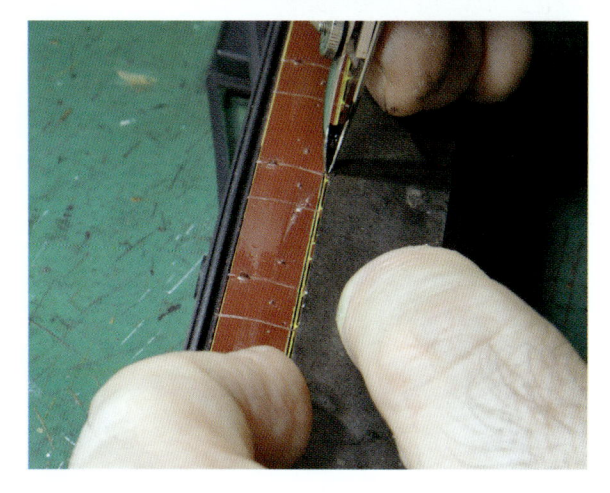

LINING

After painting the bottom and waist line, turn the model around and paint the top two lines. One line was sufficient to go directly between the two yellow lines.

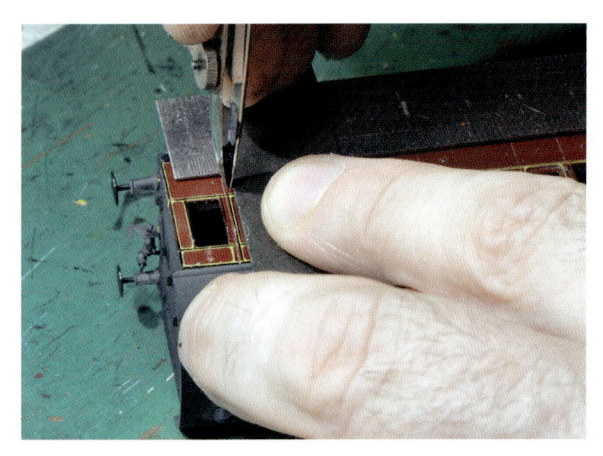

The vertical lines tend to be wider black lines, so a black line is painted adjacent to each yellow line, with this underneath the ruler. Again, work along one side, then turn it around to do the opposite lines.

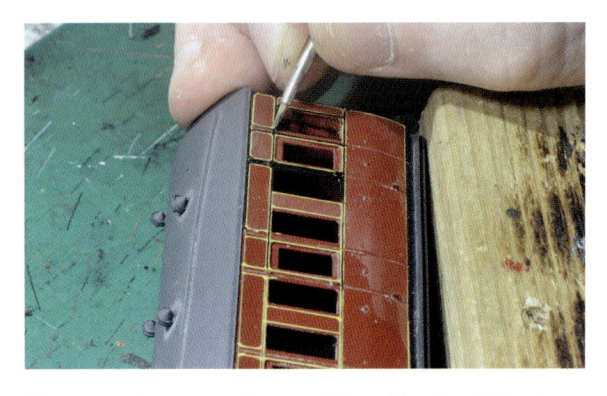

The curved corners then need brushing in, following the yellow curves already painted. The wooden block is ideal to rest on, lifting your hand to just above the height of the paint surface.

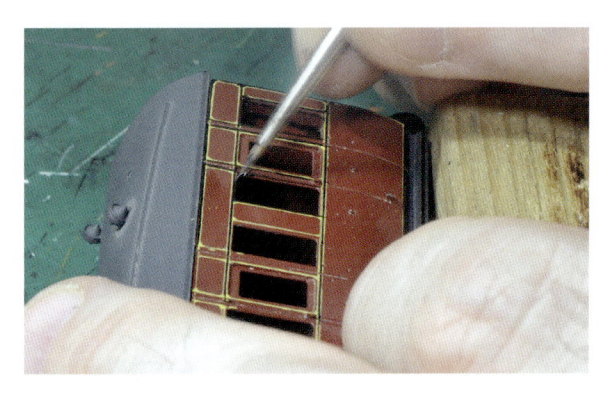

There is no yellow directly adjacent to the windows, so this can be filled in with a fine brush.

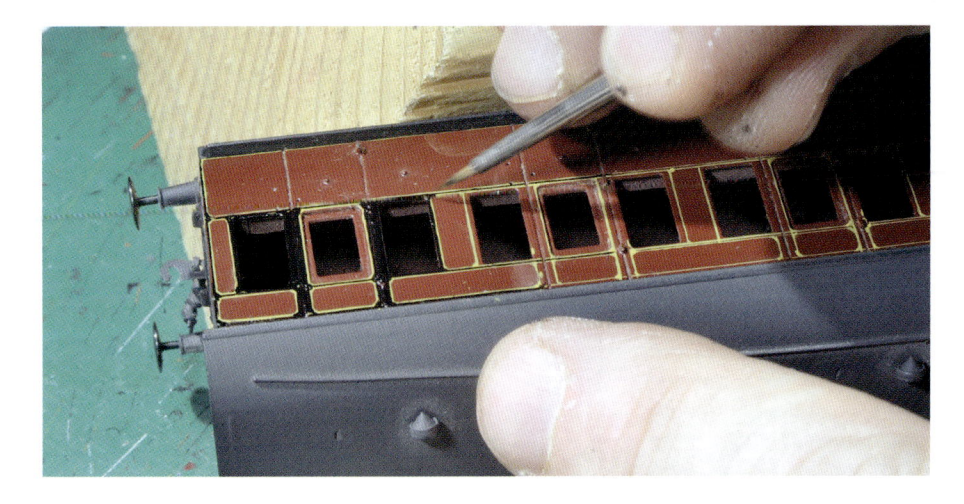

Finally, review progress, and tidy the corners with a white spirit-moistened brush as before.

LINING 89

This 4mm scale ex-LNER buffet coach has a simple yellow–black–yellow strip along its length. The actual position was referenced from a photograph of the prototype, passing just below the top of the grab handles. Two yellow lines were painted first, followed by the black down the centre. A little brush work was needed to take the lines up to and under the grab handles.

LINING LOCOMOTIVES

INSET LINING

The first step when inset lining is to mark on the model where the lines need to be positioned. There are various sources of reference, some quoting the measurement of the inset from the edge, but this should be considered along with photos of the prototype. On some models, the rivets are in the correct position, and can also be used as a guide, again with reference to photographs.

With a pair of dividers, make a light mark in the surface of the paint where the line is to be painted. Practise doing this on your test sheet – very little pressure is needed to produce a light scratch that is just visible when you go back with the bow pen. Do this at either end of the line, and for all the lines. Then, with the dividers set to the distance between the two lines, put a similar mark next to the first for the inner line.

The next step is to apply the paint. With the pen loaded and tried out on the test piece, line the ruler up with the marks for the outer line first, then the inner line. Do not stop too short; it is easier to take out lines that are too long than to add to lines that are too short. Aim to end up with the horizontal and vertical lines crossing at each end. If the marks are accurate, and the ruler is lined up correctly on these marks, the lines will be parallel, but I just like to see them forming as parallel as I paint the second line. I do the horizontal lines first, as these are the most prominent, then I do the vertical lines. I have made a small plasticard spacer that fits easily between the upper and lower pairs of lines. This raises the ruler above the surface, so the wet horizontal lines are not damaged whilst the vertical lines are being painted.

If at any point one of the lines is not consistent, or otherwise is not as good as the others, it is easy to remove them with some white spirit, a paintbrush and some kitchen towel. In this situation, it is easier to take out both lines than to take out just one line without affecting the parallel line.

Depending on the model, it may be possible to turn it over and do the other side without damaging the wet lines. If there are handrails or other items of detail that will raise the model off the flat freshly lined surface, then the other side can be lined now. I can generally line both sides of a loco or a tender on one fill of the pen.

With the straight lines on, the next step is the corners. Set the dividers to the radius of the curve of the corner. In this case it is 4 inches (it is 3 inches for the Great Western version of lined green livery). Make a very slight mark in the outer line at the point where the curve starts, then paint in the curve with the lining paintbrush. It will be thicker than required, but the focus should be on getting the curve in the right place. I normally leave the overrun of straight lines in place whilst I paint in the curves, as I find they help me to position the curve correctly.

Time now for a cup of tea or coffee, or even a proper lunch break. The point is that it is slightly easier if the paint has just started to dry slightly before embarking on the cleaning-up stage. This stage can easily take at least as long as it took to put the lines on. The excess of the straight lines need to be removed and the curves thinned and tidied. Take a fine brush and put some white spirit in a pot. Wet the brush with the white spirit, then all but dry it off on some kitchen towel. Gently stroke one side of the curve where you want to make it thinner. After the first few strokes, you will see the line start to thin. The brush is effectively blotting and drawing up the paint. Clean the brush on the kitchen towel, so that you can see how much paint has been absorbed, then re-wet the brush with the white spirit and repeat the process. Keep going until the excess straight lines have gone and the curves are smooth, and match the width of the straight lines.

Using dividers, and the bottom of the tender as a reference, make a very faint scratch mark where the top line is to be placed. Do this at both ends. The mark can be seen only when very close and in good light, and will be covered by the line when it is painted on. Repeat this for the bottom line and the outer vertical lines. Reference to photographs will help to position the lines correctly.

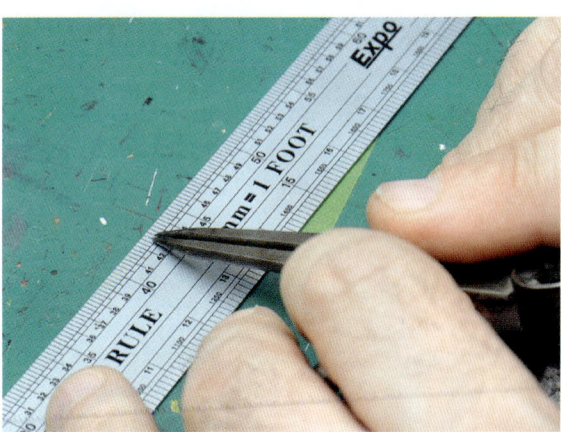

Using a scale rule, set the dividers to the distance between the two orange lines, then mark out where the parallel lines will go on the model.

Starting with the outer line, find the marks at either end. Check that the bow pen will put the line exactly over the mark by putting a dot of paint in place at either end, then paint the line in one stroke. Should a slight gap occur (if the paint stops momentarily), keep moving and finish the line, then come back and paint the missed bit with the bow pen.

LINING 91

To paint the adjacent line, start with the outer line, so that you can check that the second one is parallel as it is painted. This will prevent any damage to the line that you have just painted.

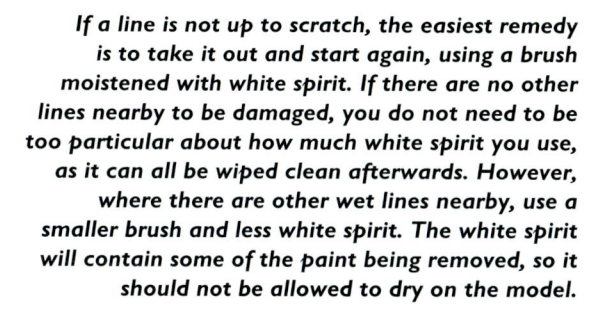

If a line is not up to scratch, the easiest remedy is to take it out and start again, using a brush moistened with white spirit. If there are no other lines nearby to be damaged, you do not need to be too particular about how much white spirit you use, as it can all be wiped clean afterwards. However, where there are other wet lines nearby, use a smaller brush and less white spirit. The white spirit will contain some of the paint being removed, so it should not be allowed to dry on the model.

The process is repeated for the bottom lines.

A spacer made from plasticard with a couple of thicker squares glued on. The squares allow it to be picked up with tweezers, and also provide a surface for the ruler to sit on. The spacer fits between the horizontal lines, and will raise the ruler so that it does not damage the wet horizontal lines whilst the vertical lines are painted.

Close-up showing that the vertical lines have now been added, meeting up with the horizontal lines.

LINING

The dividers have been set to the radius of the curves that form the corners of the panel. In this livery it is 3 inches, or 1mm in 4mm scale. A very small nick in the paint is made, to mark where each curve will start or finish.

With a lining brush, paint in the curve between the two nicks. Work with the brush on the inside of the curve; from this side, your wrist can more naturally form a curve from the inside. Do not worry if it is too thick at this stage, as this will be taken care of later. At this point, you can still see where the lines crossed. I like to leave them in to help me to frame the curve.

With a clean brush, moistened with white spirit and then blotted on kitchen towel, draw the brush along the edge of the curve. This will tidy the edge, remove any unevenness, and thin the line. Keep blotting the brush on the kitchen towel to remove the paint, and re-moisten and blot again. Also, take out the excess of the straight lines using the same method.

The black line can be added, ideally when the orange lines are dry (although it is possible straight after the orange, as there is a gap between the orange and the black). One line, about 0.35mm wide in 4mm scale, and 0.6mm wide in 7mm scale, can be painted centrally between the two orange lines. What is important is that the green is noticeable between the black and the orange, and equal on both sides.

LEFT: *After painting the horizontal black, paint the vertical.*

TIDYING LINING

The tidying stage is particularly important. Over the years I have been lining, I have seen my bow pen lining and my brush work improve, but the area in which I have improved the most is probably the tidying and cleaning. The secret is to use a tiny amount of white spirit on the brush, having blotted it on some kitchen towel before taking it to the area to be tidied. If you are taking out part of a line that has been over-painted (such as the corner that will become a curve), then stroke the paint with the brush from above. If it is a line that needs to be smoothed or thinned, draw the brush along the side of the line. Blot the brush on the kitchen towel and you will see the paint soak off the brush. Moisten and blot again, then repeat. Take your time and keep it as local to the line as possible. Any marks left are normally paint that has been moved from the line and not picked up. If necessary, a gentle rub with a cocktail stick will remove anything stubborn. A gloss finish is a lot easier to clean than a satin or a matt finish.

When the orange lines are dry (normally 24 hours later), the black line can be painted in the middle. This line is 1 inch wide on the prototype and should have half an inch of green either side. Again, start with the horizontal lines, then the vertical lines. This time, use the orange curves as a guide of where to stop, then brush in the curves at the corner. If necessary, you can tidy the black corner in the same way as the orange. However, as the line is thicker than the orange, it is quite easy to paint the black line without the need for tidying afterwards.

CURVES, VALENCES AND SPLASHERS

There are three options when lining curves:

- A template can be made for the curve, and the bow pen drawn round to paint the line.
- The bow pen attached to the pair of compasses can be used to follow a parallel edge.
- The curve can be painted in with a lining brush and tidied afterwards.

Templates can work well and I have used this approach on the curves at the front of the A4. The pattern was drawn by hand, with close reference to photographs, then the template was cut from plasticard. I have also made some templates for splashers on occasions, but they need to be made first, which takes a little time. Also, in my experience there is a limit to the extent of the radius through which you can neatly turn a bow pen. I have tried painting the curved corners at the end of the straight lines on tender lining with a bow pen, but I found that the result was no better than brushing them.

The second is probably my preferred option for painting curves, but the method does depend on two aspects. First, the line must be parallel to an

The black curves are brushed in as before.

Being wider than the orange, it is easier to get the black right first time with one stroke.

If the black is not right first time, it can be tidied as before.

Tender sides are perhaps slightly easier, as there are generally fewer features in the way, and more space to work. On this cab side, the top horizontal lines are very close to the small handrail.

The verticals are quite straightforward.

edge that can be followed with the other leg of the compass. Second, there must be space for the bow pen and the compass to access the area where the curve needs to be painted.

If neither of the first two methods is suitable – which may be the case where there is a space issue – then brushing in the curve is the only option left. It requires a very steady hand and the most amount of tidying up afterwards.

BORDER LINING

The process of painting border lining is not dissimilar to that for inset lining. In some respects, it is simpler, as it is generally more obvious where the line is to be positioned. Also, corners tend to be square rather than curved. However, in other respects it is more complex, as there can be more curves to follow than with inset lining. Often, border lining consists of at least two colours. Start with the most prominent. If

LINING

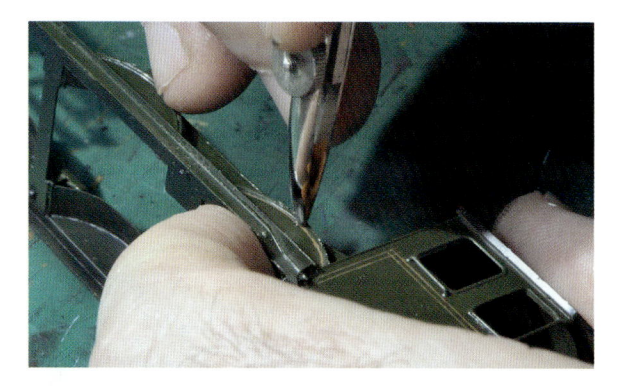

On this 4mm scale Castle, it is possible to let the bow pen follow the raised beading when painting the lining on to the splasher. Otherwise, a template or the bow pen and compasses would be needed.

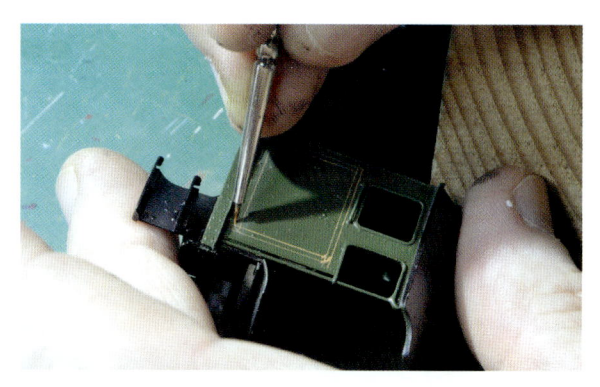

With the straight lines painted, the curves are brushed in, then tidied.

The lower front curve has a much larger radius, so is much longer. With the small step part way round, a template or the bow pen with compasses are not really practical, so the curve was brushed in.

With both lines in place, the tidying can be done. Draw the white spirit-moistened brush along the sides of the lines to thin them and smooth the edges.

Brushing is particularly difficult but, with time taken to tidy the lines, the result can match the lines drawn with the bow pen.

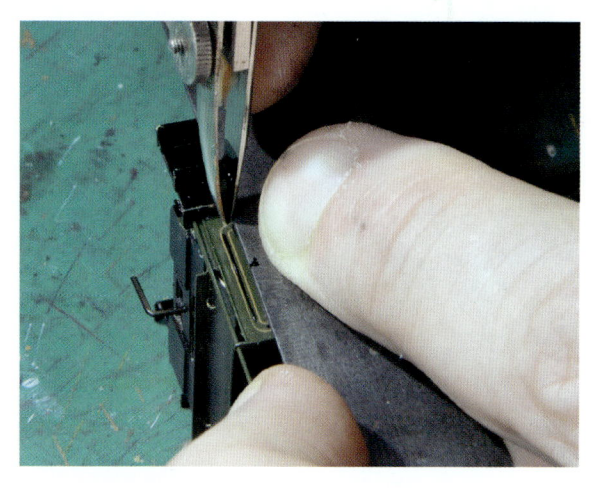

The black lines are again added centrally between the orange lines, horizontal first, then vertical.

With the straight lines painted, the curves can be brushed in.

Work round each corner in turn.

Again, the black line is easier on the longer curve, although a little bit of thinning will be required.

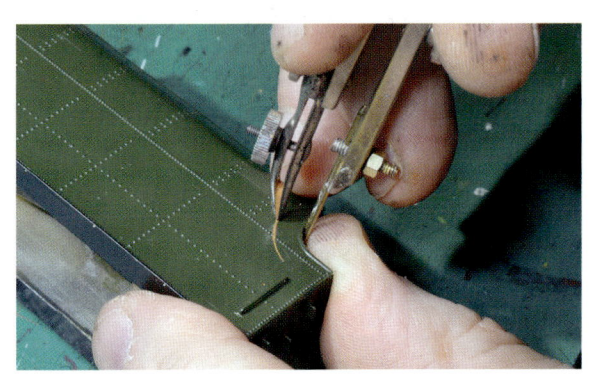

With curves such as these on this 4mm scale Stanier tender, the bow pen and compasses set-up comes into its own. The curves are parallel with the edge of the tender side.

If the bow pen travels over any rivets, the width of the line will change either side. This can be taken care of during the tidying.

Draw the white spirit-moistened brush along the edge of the line at the wide point, and thin the line until it is consistent with the rest.

LINING 97

After a few strokes, the line will be down to the required width.

Here, the bow pen and compasses are being used to paint the line on to the valence of this 4mm scale Duchess.

RIGHT: *The curve for the front of an A4 was drawn on to paper first, with close reference to photographs of the prototype. The paper template was placed on to the model to check it for accuracy, then plasticard templates were cut out from it. Both sides of the cut plasticard were used, one for the outer line, and one for the inner line, to paint curves on to transfer paper.*

A 7mm scale A4. The Garter Blue livery has a red line adjacent to the black front, then a blue gap, and a parallel white line.

LINING

The bow pen and compasses are ideal for this border lining, following the edge of the tender side. The yellow is painted first, then the black is added using the same method when the yellow is fully dry. As the black is trimming the yellow, it would be wise to allow at least two days for the yellow to dry.

After the black line has been painted, the space to the edge of the tender can be brushed in.

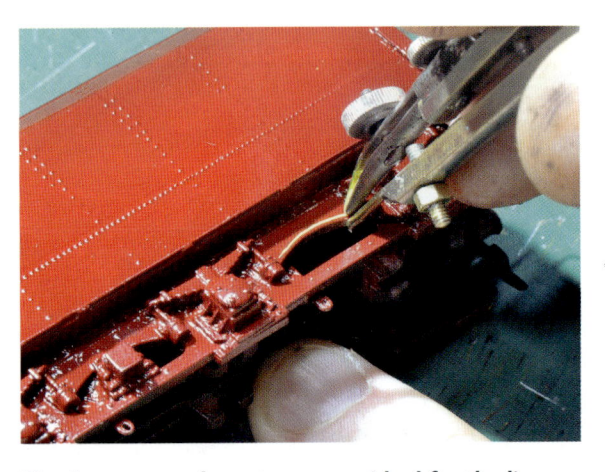

The bow pen and compasses are ideal for the lines on this 4mm scale ex-LMS tender.

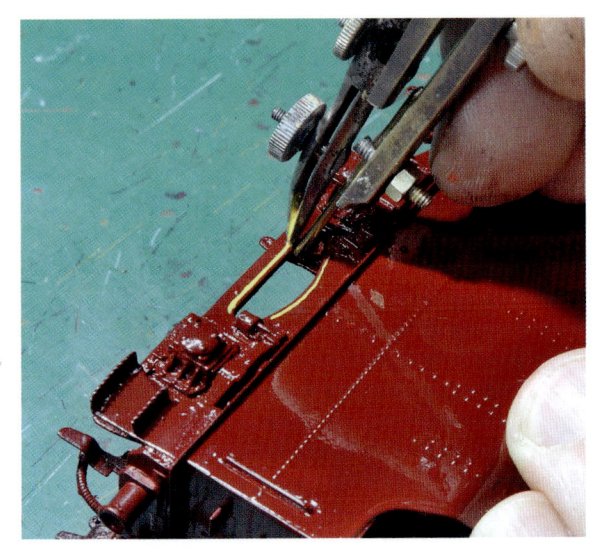

There are a lot of lines to be painted here. The bottom edge will also receive yellow and black lines.

The bow pen will not get right up to the obstacles, so the last part of the line needs to be brushed in.

The sides of the tender step backing plate also needs lining; the same approach can be used.

LINING 99

The black line trims the outer edge of the yellow line.

any colours are particularly wide, once the line has been painted in adjacent to its neighbouring colour with the bow pen and dried, the gap to the edge of the panel can be filled in with a brush.

BOILER BANDS

Sometimes, access with a bow pen is nearly or completely impossible, for example, where boiler bands are needed, or lines on certain features such as buffer beams, tank fronts and some tender or bunker rears. This may be because there are detail items in the way, such as lamp irons and vac pipes, or it could be that there is just not enough space to get the pen in. In these situations, I do the same lines on to transfer paper and, when it is dry, apply the lining as with a transfer.

Making such lining transfers is a good place to start before putting the bow pen on the model. Start with a blank piece of transfer paper. This is produced by a small number of manufacturers and available from various model suppliers. First, spray the main body colour directly on to the paper. Use either acrylic or enamel paint, but not cellulose, as the latter can damage the paper. This step is needed in case there is a gap between the lines and also to provide some additional strength to the transfer. Very little of this colour will show on the finished model, so it does not matter if it is not the same paint as has been used on the rest of it. For example,

I use a cellulose green for GWR/BR locomotives but, for the boiler bands, I use an enamel green on the transfer paper. The boiler bands consist of two orange lines, with a black line between them. There should be a small amount of green visible between the orange and the black.

Once the base colour has dried, normally the next day in the case of enamels, mark on the paper exactly where the lines need to be painted. This is normally in the form of a pair of indentations on either end of where the line is going, with a pair of dividers set to the width of the boiler bands required. The lines can then be painted simply with the bow pen and a ruler. If a second or third colour is required, these can be added once the first colour has dried. Having said that, in the case of orange–black–orange boiler bands, I have been known to put the black line down the middle straight after the orange, if I have not wanted to wait the extra day. The fact that the lines do not touch is critical in that situation; it is merely a case of ensuring that the ruler is sitting above the wet orange lines.

This is an ideal point at which to mention transfer fixers and softeners, which are used to help transfers to adhere to surfaces. If the surface is not completely flat – for example, if it needs to sit over some rivets – then a softener will help the transfer to fit over and around the rivets, giving the impression of being painted on, rather than sitting over. I use Micro Set and Micro Sol from the Micro Scale range, which works well with the transfer paper from the same manufacturer.

Once the boiler bands have been painted on to the transfer sheet, they can be fitted to the model. Using a scrap of paper cut into a strip, measure the length of the boiler band by wrapping the strip around the boiler, then use this as a template to cut the boiler band to the required length. With a sharp blade, cut very close to the painted line on each side. A light cut is all that is needed to cut through the transfer layer – you only need to cut right through the backing paper on one side to separate the transfer from the sheet.

Soak the boiler band in some water according

100 LINING

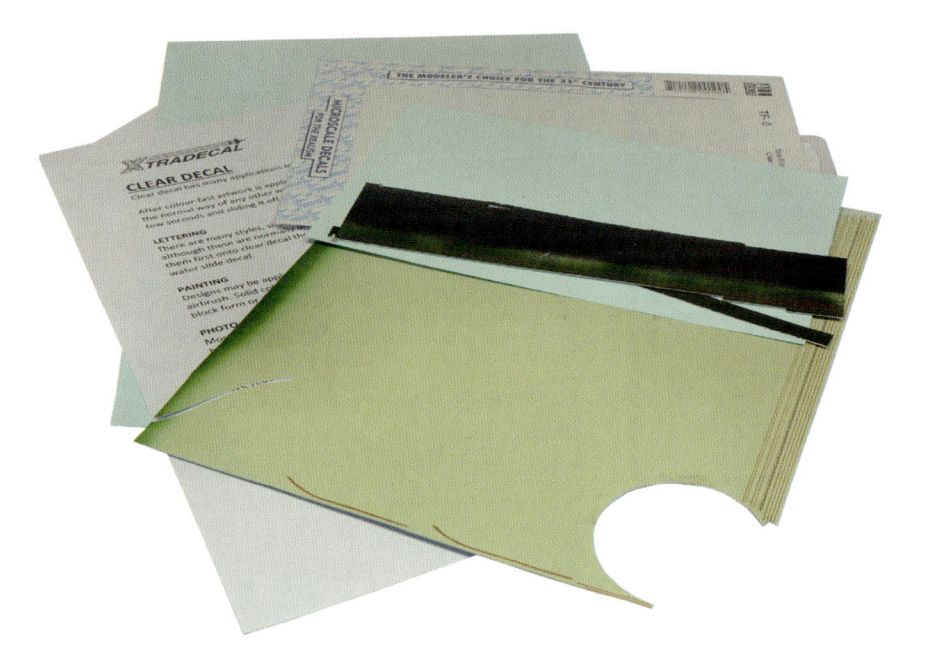

Various sheets of transfer paper, from Fox, Microscale and Xtradecal.

to the instructions of the transfer paper and, if using a fixer, apply some with a brush to the place where the transfer is required. After soaking, carefully slide the boiler band sideways off the backing paper and on to the surface of the model. Carefully manoeuvre it into position with a cocktail stick or a pair of tweezers. Once it is generally in place, apply a slight pulling motion along its length to help it to straighten. There is no need to rush this stage. If it starts to dry, drop some water on to the surface.

Keep checking that the boiler band is straight, and perpendicular to the length of the boiler. When you are satisfied, move on to the next boiler band; when a second and a third are added, it will become more apparent if one of them is not straight or perpendicular. If at this point you find that one of the boiler bands applied earlier needs to be adjusted and has now dried, applying some more Micro Set will allow it to be manoeuvred slightly, or lifted and repositioned.

First, the transfer paper needs to be sprayed with the main body colour. This is best done with enamel, as cellulose can cause damage.

Once the transfer paper is fully dry, lines can be painted on with the bow pen.

LINING

BR/GWR boiler bands painted up on transfer paper.

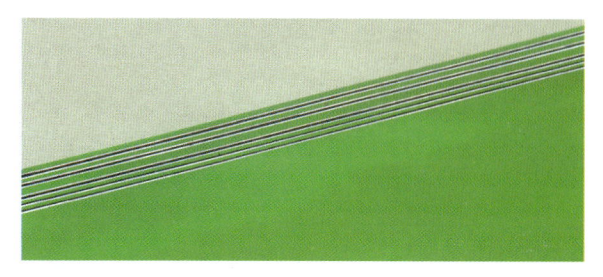

LNER/GNR boiler bands.

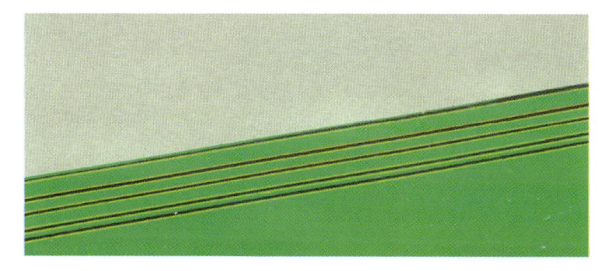

SR boiler bands.

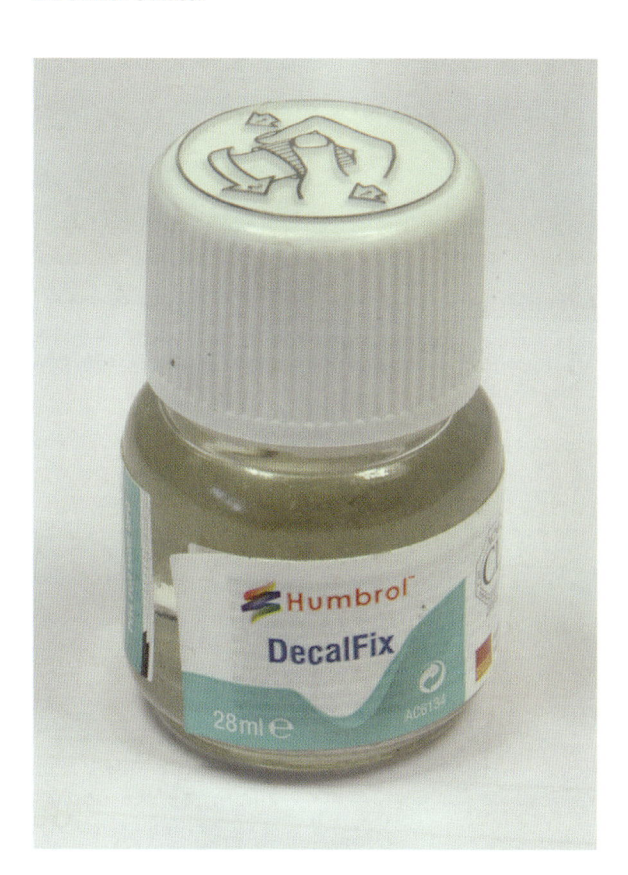

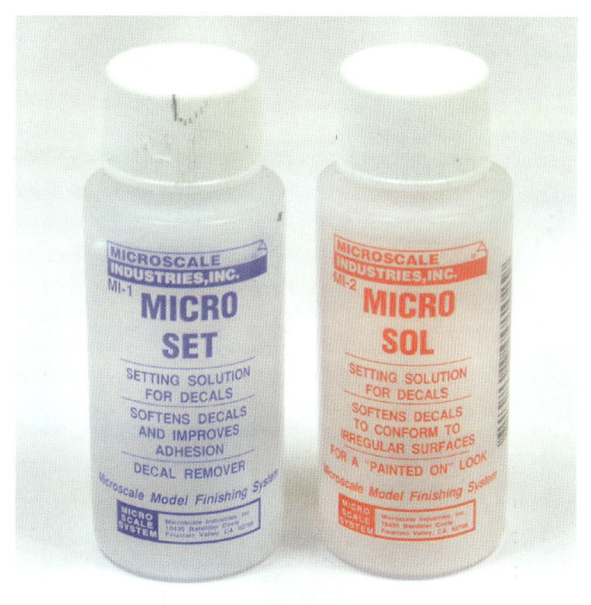

Micro Set and Micro Sol products are very helpful when putting on transfers, particularly if the surface is not completely flat.

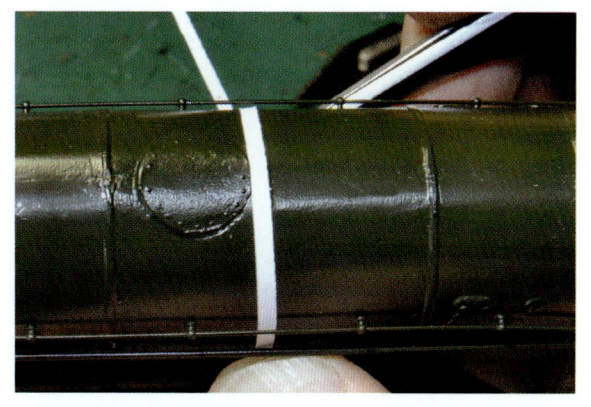

There are other solutions available for helping to fix transfers.

To create a boiler band, a strip is cut from a sheet of paper, then placed on the model and cut to the required length.

LINING

The strip is then used to cut a boiler band from the transfer paper.

Cut accurately along the edge of the orange.

Whilst the boiler band is soaking in some water, apply some Micro Set to the area where the boiler band will be placed.

Remove the transfer from the water and place it on the model close to where it needs to go, then slide it off the backing paper. Move it into position with a cocktail stick.

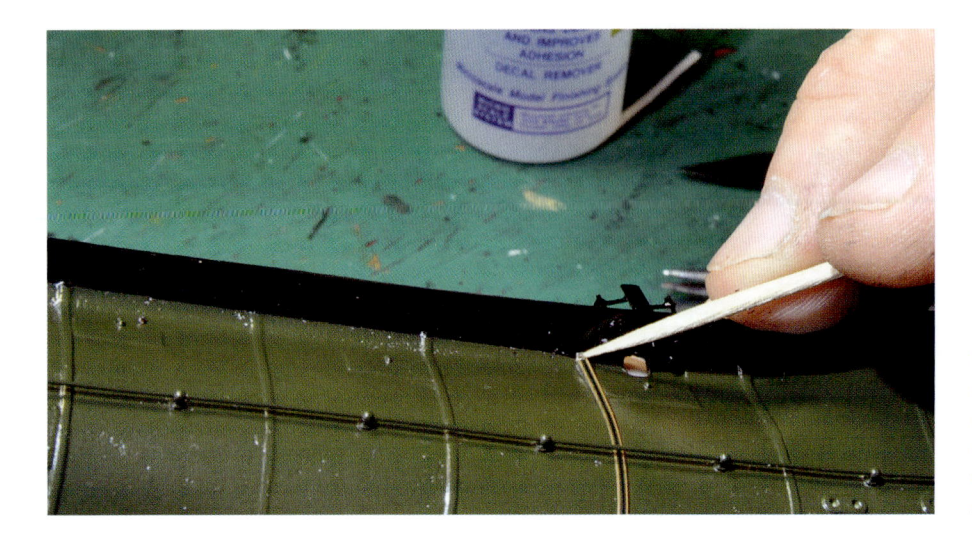

When the transfer is in the right place, apply a slight pulling action with the cocktail stick to either end, to help straighten it.

CYLINDERS AND OTHER DIFFICULT AREAS

The process for cylinder wrappers is the same, but with the additional application of some softener to take care of the rivets. Apply Micro Set in the same way as with the boiler bands, then, once the transfer is in position, apply some Micro Sol to the top surface. Leave it for a few minutes to work. Sometimes, the transfer looks as if it has wrinkled up, and it is tempting to start prodding with a cocktail stick, but this is just the softener working. Within a few minutes, the transfer will have sunk down, so that it is sitting fully on the surface of the model, and the wrinkles will have disappeared.

The approach of painting the lining on to transfer paper can also be used in other difficult areas where access with a pen is not possible. As the same paint is used, the lining will match that which has been painted directly on to the model.

Some buffer beams require border lining. With little space around the buffers, and with vacuum pipes and steam pipes obstructing the length of the buffer beam, applying the lining straight on with a pen is very challenging. Transfers can be trimmed if necessary with a sharp craft knife to fit around the buffers and up to vacuum pipes, to look like the lines continue underneath.

The front of tanks is another area that often carries lining, but is very difficult to access. Again, a painted transfer is ideal. I have also used this approach for the lower horizontal line on the back of tenders and tanks, and matched them in with the vertical lines painted on directly.

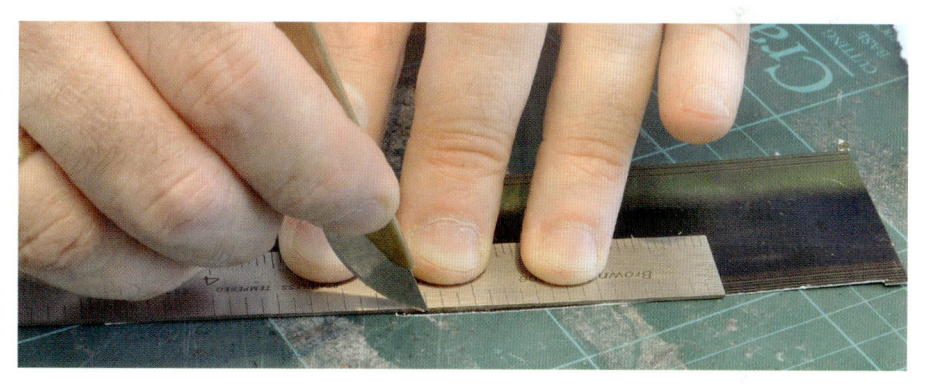

Cut right on the edge of the lining.

Micro Set also works as part of a two-stage process when the surface is uneven, such as over rivets.

Position the lining on the cylinder cover.

LINING

The bow pen and compasses being loaded with paint, ready to line some wheels. One drop of paint from the cocktail stick is sufficient.

With the wheel mounted on to the tool, and the tool held in the vice, the line around the rim can be painted.

The wheel centre also has a line. Once the distance on the compasses has been set, bring the pen down on to the wheel, then slowly rotate either the wheel or the compasses.

The approach with the driving wheels is exactly the same.

The Great Northern Railway painted around the whole boss, rather than a circle line around the axle. The crank pin hole can be used to locate the point of the compasses.

Now the two curves need to be joined with a brush.

LINING

Follow the edge of the boss with the brush.

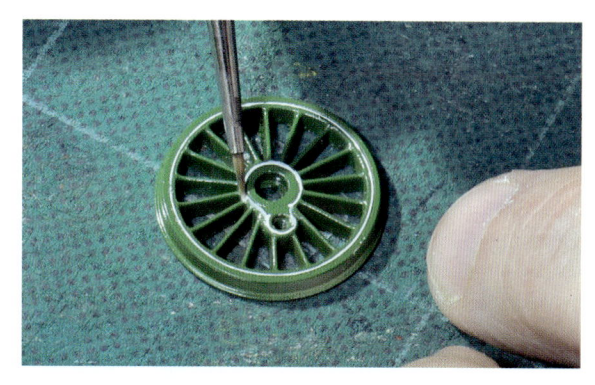

Next, tidy the brushed part of the line with a white spirit-moistened brush.

Blend the lines on either side into the curves painted with the bow pen, and take out the excess.

The white line has been finished and the model is ready for the black line.

The black is painted in the same way as the white, just trimming the width as necessary.

The finished wheel.

LINING

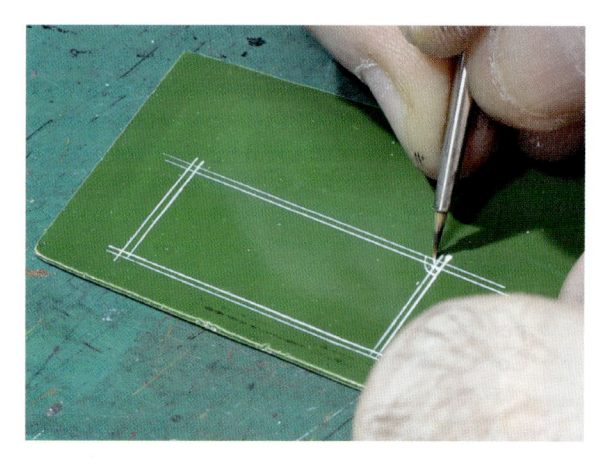

Painting in the second curve.

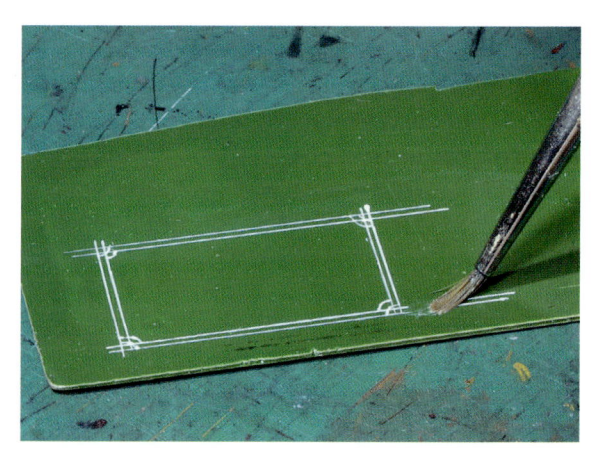

Start by cleaning away the excess lines.

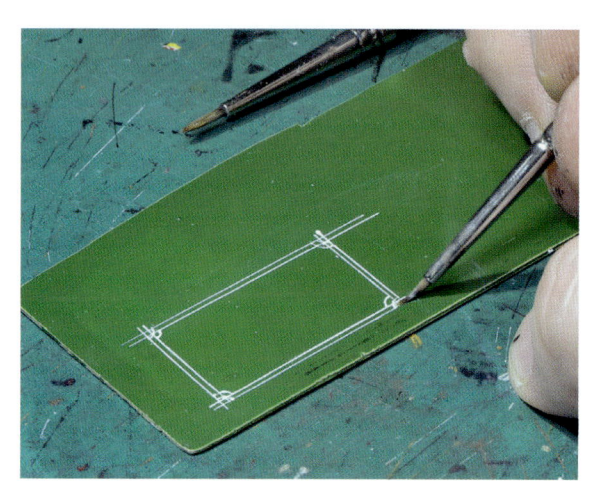

Trim the excess back to the curve.

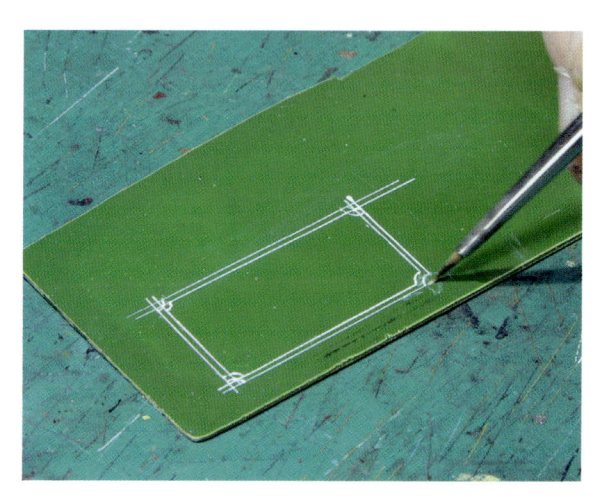

Mop up all the white marks, which are paint remnants.

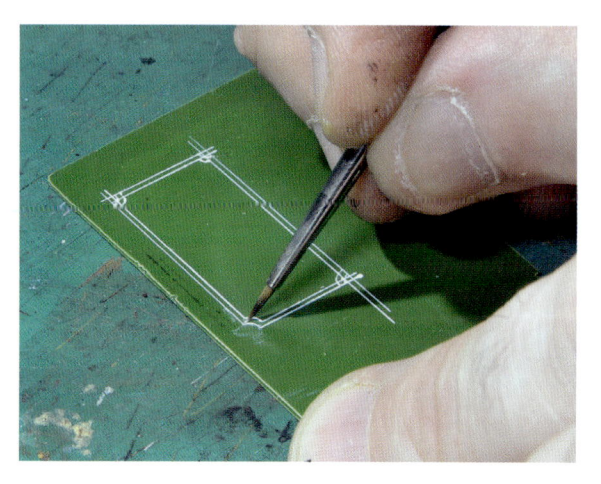

Trim the curves.

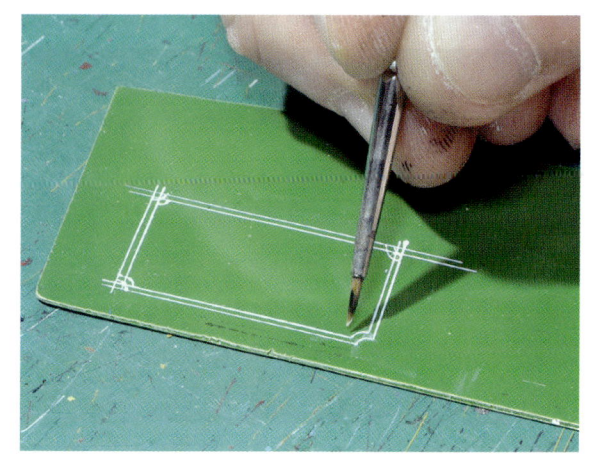

Match the width of the lines.

LINING

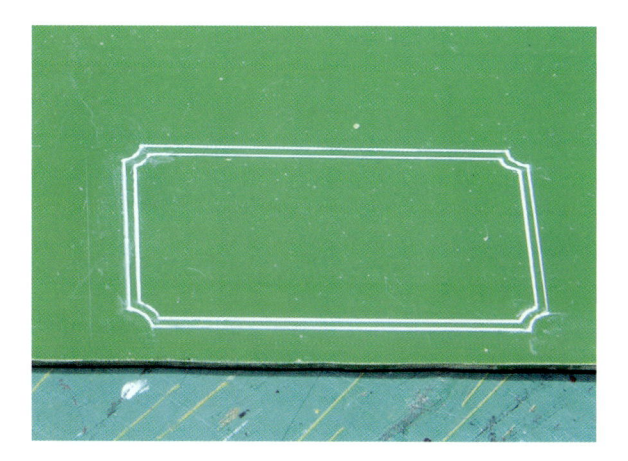

The white lines finished.

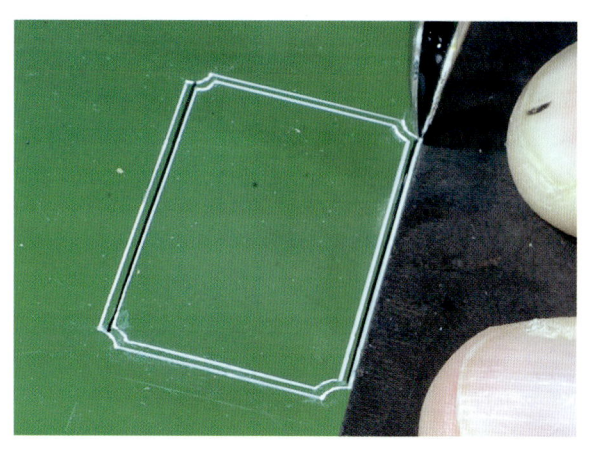

Paint the black lines on each side, with the steel rule over the adjacent white line.

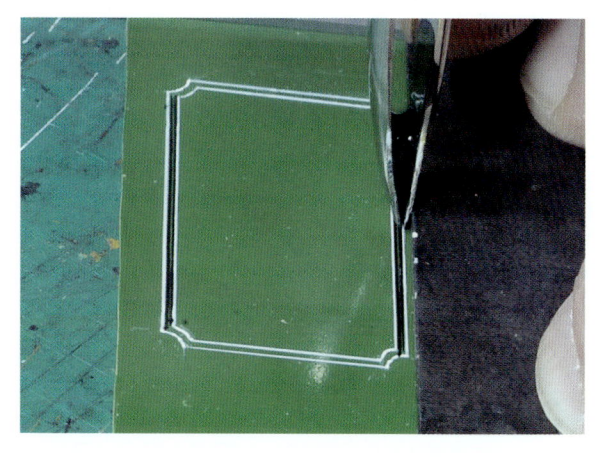

Turn the model round to paint the other side.

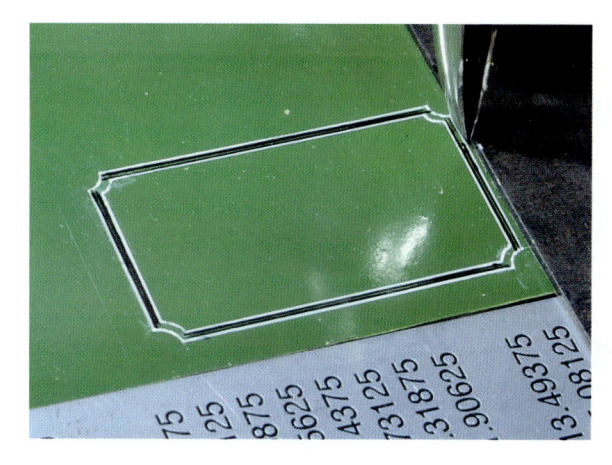

Repeat with the vertical lines.

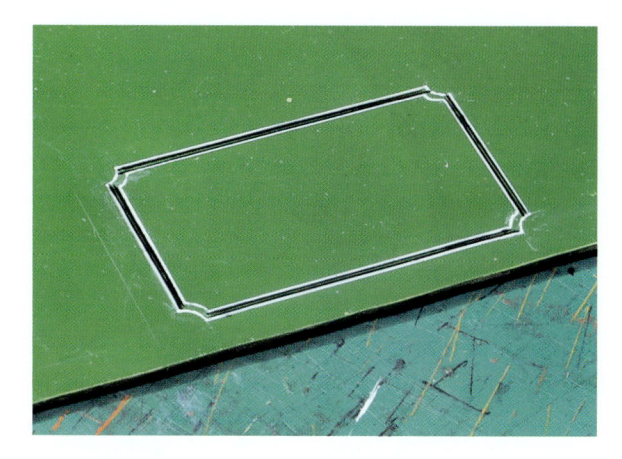

The black lines are in place, ready for the curves to be brushed in.

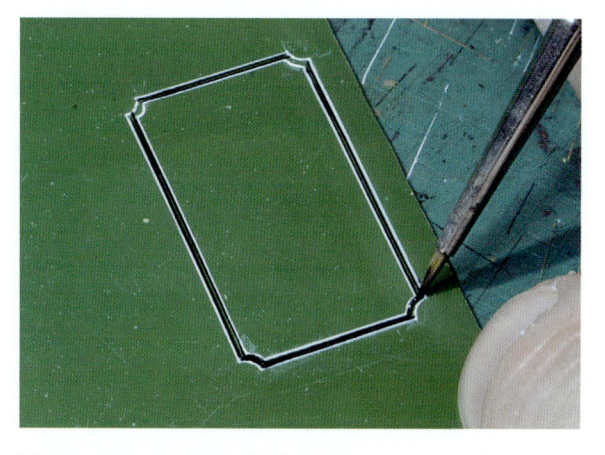

The corners can now be brushed in, as can the gap between the black lines.

LINING

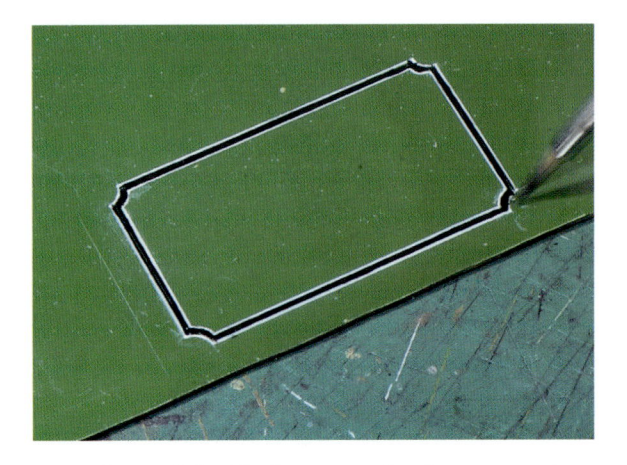

Any tidying of the black can now be done.

Next, the dark green on the outside of the panel can be added. Start by painting a line adjacent to the white with the bow pen.

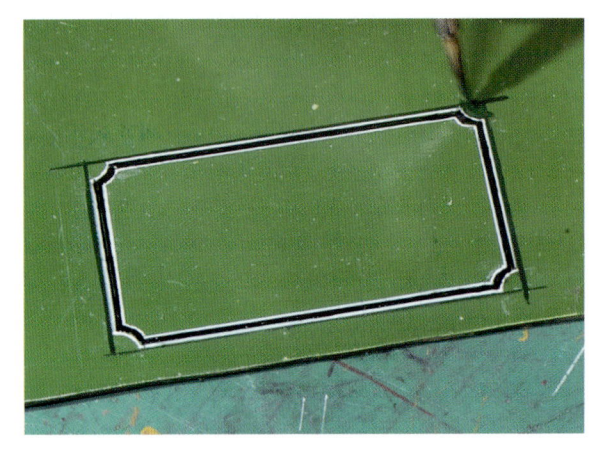

Fill in the corners with a brush.

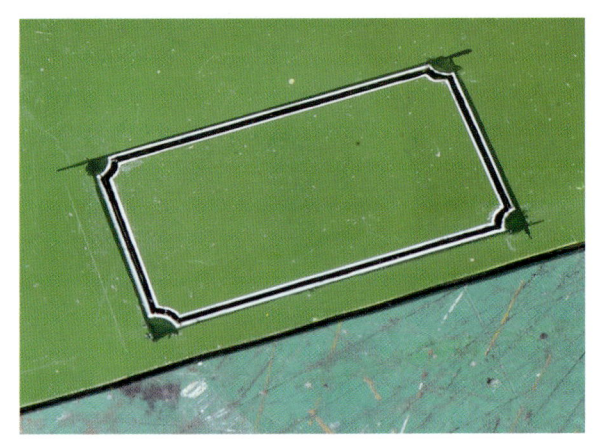

Allow the panel to dry.

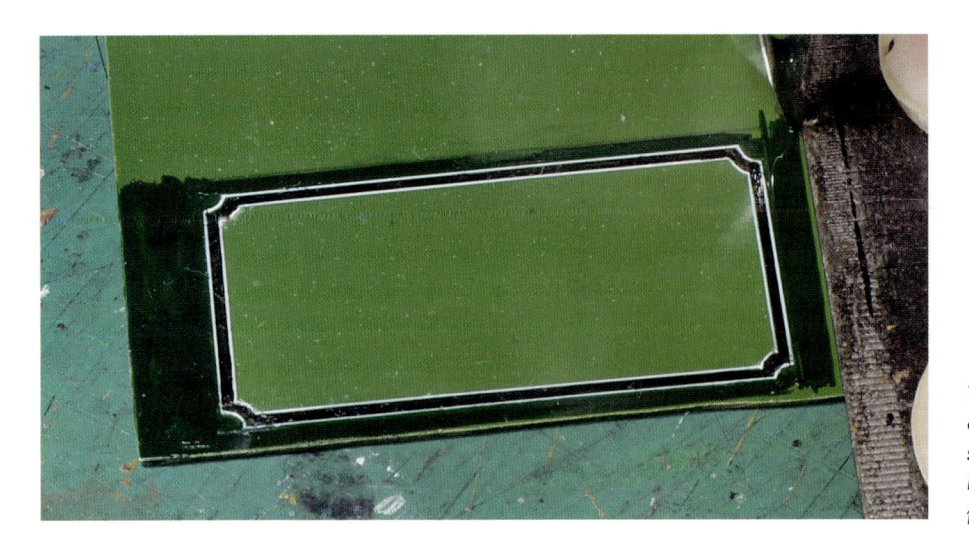

The rest of the panel can be filled in with a series of slightly wider lines with the bow pen.

LINING | 113

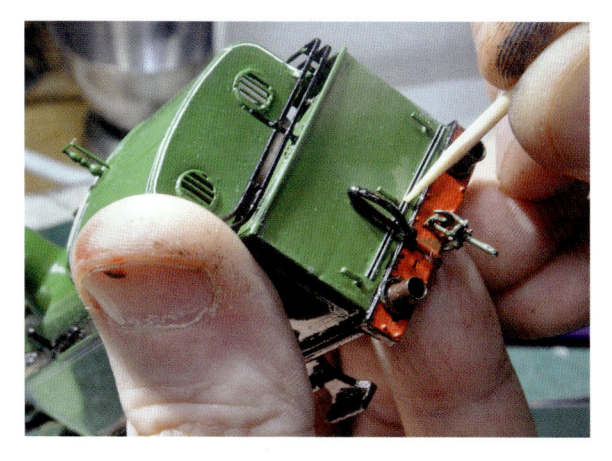

I decided to use boiler bands for the bunker rear on this model. As ever, I started with the horizontals.

Move the band into position with a cocktail stick, checking that it is at the same height as the lines on either side of the bunker.

Repeat for the second horizontal.

The verticals can be put into position next.

Repeat for the second vertical, then allow the transfer adhesive to set.

Mark where the curves for the corners start.

LINING

With a very sharp blade, and very little pressure, cut through the transfer at the mark.

Apply a little Micro Set to the part of the transfer to be removed. The product will loosen the adhesive.

After the application of the Micro Set, the unwanted part of the transfer can be removed with a cocktail stick.

The corner is now ready to be painted in.

Brush in the curves.

Once the white is in place and dried, the black can be painted in, and the dark green on the outside.

LINING | 115

The finished model, complete with wheels and chassis.

The 4mm Duchess has been lined, and is awaiting numbering and varnishing.

LINING

An unusual model – and an unusual livery.

A 7mm scale Z4. Based in Scotland, it was actually lined in the style of the Great North of Scotland Railway.

LINING 117

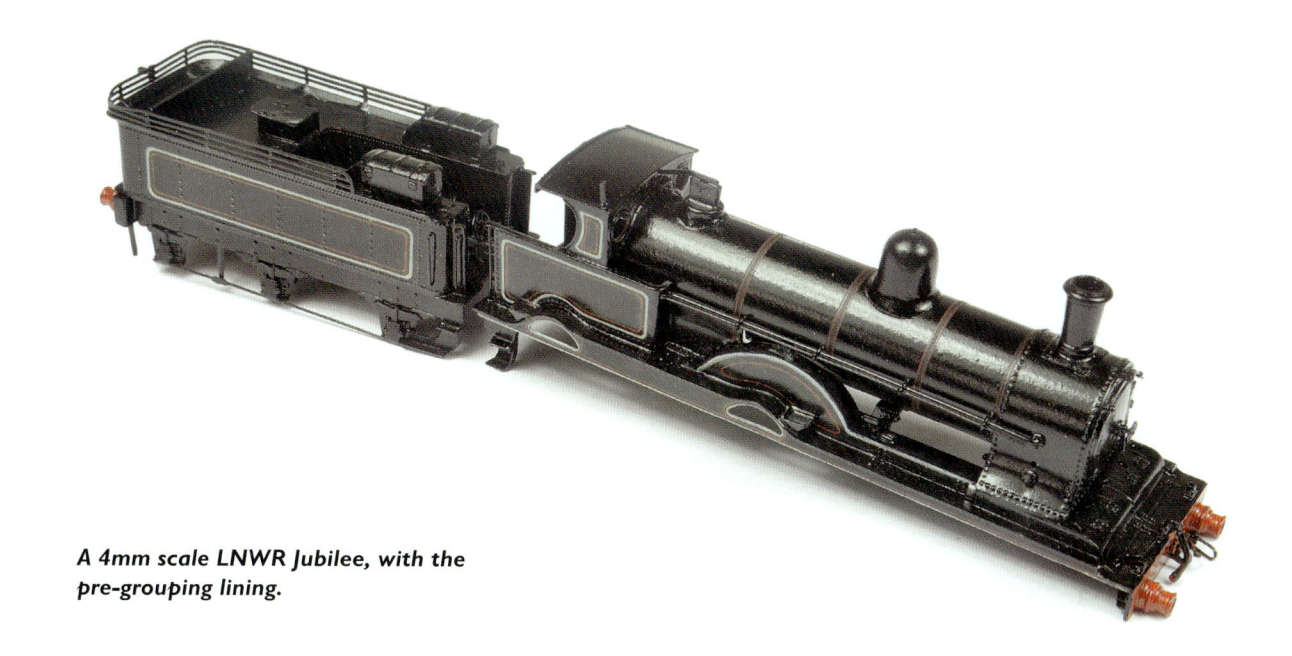

A 4mm scale LNWR Jubilee, with the pre-grouping lining.

The LNWR livery in a larger scale. This is a gauge 2 model.

LINING

ABOVE: **The GWR livery was slightly different from the BR express Passenger Green livery. The valence was black in GWR days and the lining was more ornate on the cab side and the cab front. This model was painted by Alan Brackenborough.**

The lining around the cab front was brushed in on this 4mm scale Castle.

LINING 119

The lining on the cab side of this 4mm scale B17 needed to be positioned carefully. Photographs of the prototype show that there was not much room to fit the lining and the large numbers.

Completed M&SWJR 4-4-4.

Loco livery displaying both inset and border lining.

120 LINING

The finished M&SWJR 2-6-0.

A 7mm scale GWR steam railmotor on the work bench, part way through the lining process. The lines below the waist have been painted; just the upper black verticals to go.

The completed model.

CHAPTER EIGHT

ADDING LETTERING AND NUMBERS, AND VARNISHING

Once your model has been painted, and the lining has been applied if appropriate, the model takes another step towards coming to life, with the addition of lettering, numbering and any crests. Good-quality transfers are available for the vast majority of railway vehicles from the big four railway companies and post nationalization. There is also quite a wide selection of transfers available for pre-grouping railway companies. However, occasionally something is required for which transfers are not available, and some hand painting will be needed.

The next stage in the process is the application of a coat of varnish to the model, which will give some protection to any transfers. It will also adjust the tone. The majority, if not all, of the paint applied up to now will have been gloss, and even a showcase model is likely to need to have the level of gloss brought down a little with a varnish.

USING TRANSFERS

TYPES OF TRANSFER AVAILABLE

There are four types of transfer available. The Historical Model Railway Society (HMRS) has quite an extensive range in both 4mm and 7mm scales.

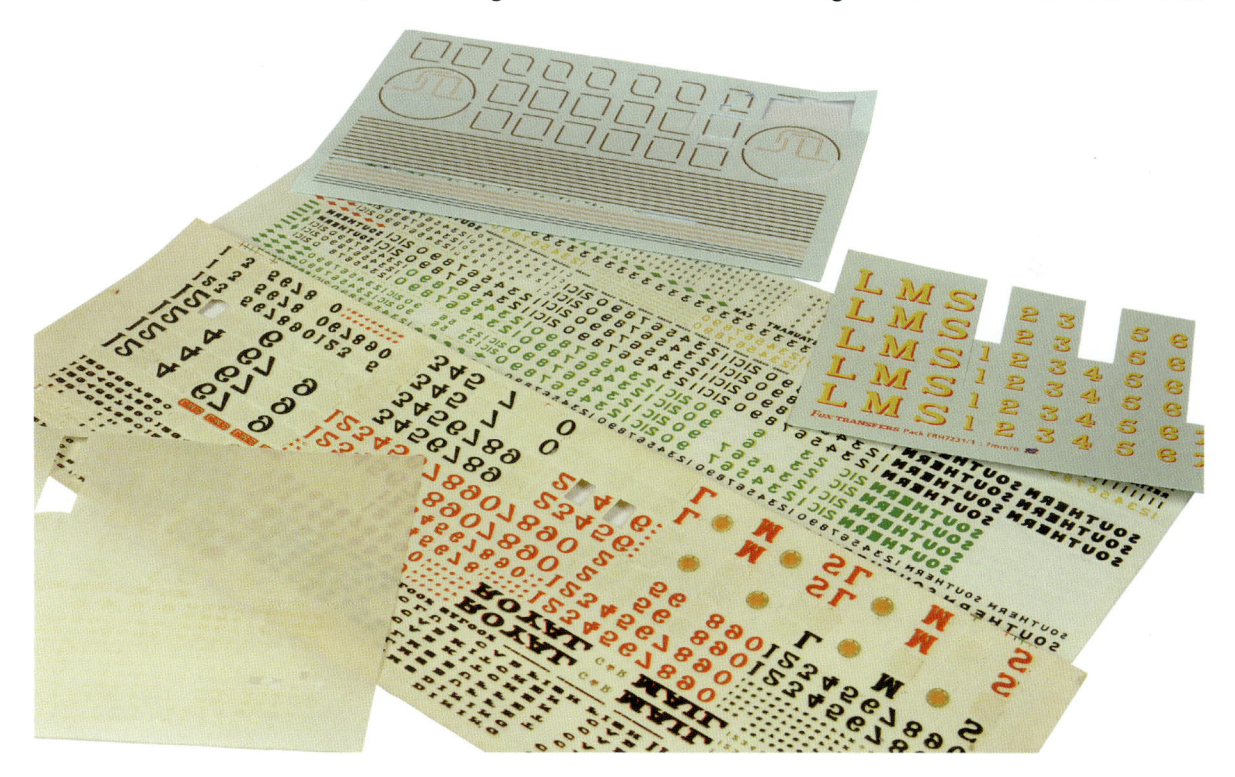

A sample of the various types of transfer available: in front with the protective sheet is Pressfix, then Methfix, without the protective sheet. Behind are two sheets of waterslide transfers.

They come in two types: Pressfix and Methfix. Waterslide transfers are available from a number of suppliers, some of whom have quite diverse ranges. Finally, there are the 'rub-down' transfers, which are applied dry. I make extensive use of both types of HMRS transfer as well as a variety of waterslide transfers. I have encountered rub-down transfers on only a few occasions.

The HMRS transfers do not have a carrier film surrounding the actual transfer, or separating the individual letters and numbers, but sometimes they leave a residue, which needs to be cleaned off after application. Its Pressfix transfers are a little easier to use, as they are slightly adhesive, and will hold their position prior to the application of the water that is needed for permanent adhesion. Methfix transfers do not have this slight adhesion and require a mix of methylated spirit and water to activate the adhesive.

The choice of which type of transfer to use is a matter of personal preference and availability. As Pressfix is perhaps the more commonly used type, there is usually more stock of it available. Not every sheet has always been available in Methfix. Pressfix is a little easier to use, but Methfix is slightly thinner, and has a slightly more subtle appearance.

Waterslide transfers are simple to apply and easy to move into position. They are applied wet, having been soaked in water, to remove the backing paper and activate the adhesive. Decal softeners and fixers can be used with waterslide transfers.

APPLYING PRESSFIX TRANSFERS

Reference to photographs will help with the correct position of the transfer on the model, in particular the height and lateral position. Look for identifiable aspects, such as the position of rivets if possible, or line up the letters or numbers with the level of a raised footplate or the axle boxes on a tender.

Once the correct position has been identified, it can be useful to put a very small reference point on the model, using a soft pencil. This is not essential, but it may be very helpful where it is not possible to put the transfer straight into position, or if it is particularly complex.

The next stage is to cut out the transfer. Using a craft knife, cut around the whole area of the transfer needed. If it is a set of letters, such as 'LMS', unless

Make a slight mark with a pencil where the transfer is to be placed.

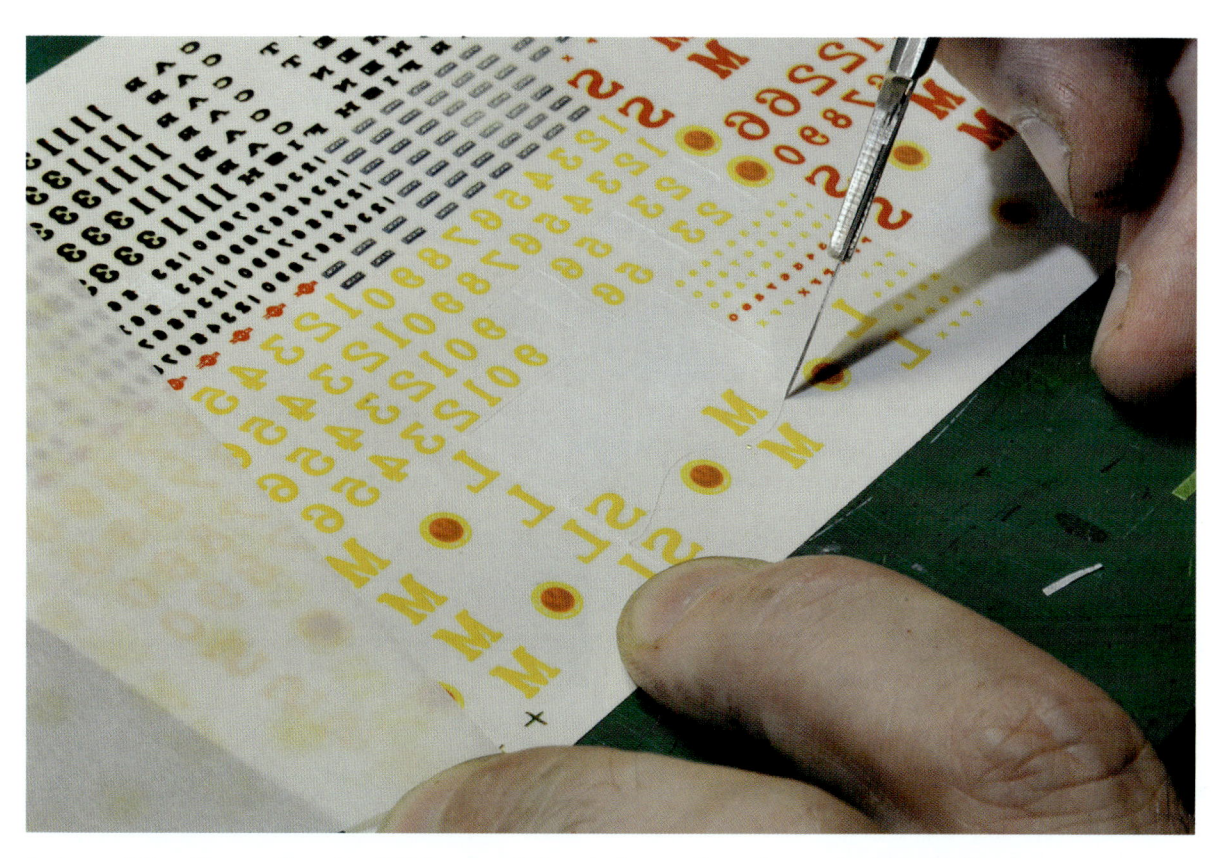

ADDING LETTERING AND NUMBERS, AND VARNISHING | 123

A sheet of Pressfix transfers. Cut lightly around the whole transfer – the cut does not need to go through the sheet, just through the carrying paper – then slide the knife under the corner of the carrying paper to separate it from the sheet. Lift with tweezers.

Line the transfer up in the approximate position, manoeuvring it with a cocktail stick. Press down lightly.

you intend to change the spacing – some locomotives did have lettering with non-standard spacing, and this is another reason why it is important to refer to photographs – cut around the whole set of letters in one go. It is not necessary to cut right through the sheet, just the thin layer that carries the transfer. Then, with a pair of tweezers or, if it is a little stubborn, the blade of a craft knife, lift and separate the transfer carrier film and place it on the model. Very little pressure is needed to press it roughly in position. To move it into its exact position, lift it very slightly with some tweezers and lightly press it again. It is important not to rush this part of the process and to check each letter carefully. Use a pair of dividers to ensure that each letter is exactly the same height from a key point, such as the footplate – assuming that the footplate is straight and level.

Once you are satisfied that everything is straight and level, carefully press each letter slightly more firmly to ensure it is secure. Check again, then apply a small amount of water to the carrier paper. This can be done by dipping your finger into an egg cup of water, then dropping this on to the transfer. After a few seconds, the carrier paper will separate from the transfer, so that it can be removed. The area can then be dried by dabbing gently with some kitchen towel.

Check the position of the first letter, using dividers, measuring from the footplate. Press down again.

Move along the transfer, ensuring that each letter or number is at the same level.

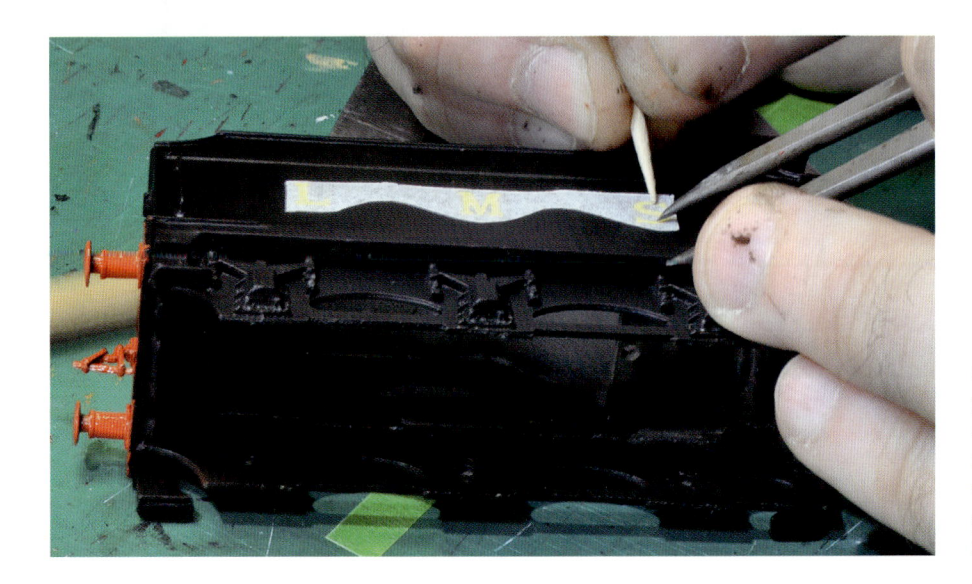

It is important to take your time with this stage, as a very slight misalignment will be very visible. Some people seem to delight in finding such errors!

ADDING LETTERING AND NUMBERS, AND VARNISHING

Once you are happy that everything is where it needs to be, apply some water, by dipping a finger and dabbing it on to the transfer. After a few seconds, the carrier film will separate from the transfer.

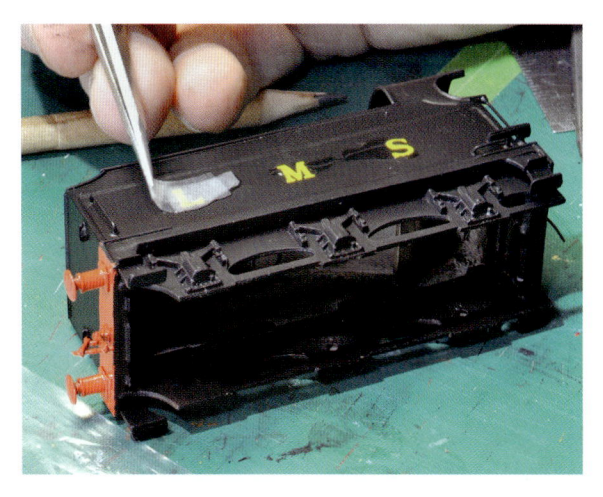

Remove the carrier film with tweezers.

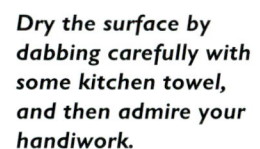

Dry the surface by dabbing carefully with some kitchen towel, and then admire your handiwork.

Numbers have the additional task of setting the spacing. This is done again with reference to photos and using a scale rule. Bear in mind that the digit 'I' has smaller spacing than other digits. However, the spacing is sometimes dictated by the model. As an example, the LMS 'Big Bertha' used on the Lickey incline had a five-digit number for some of its lifetime, which was quite a tight fit on the cab side. The easiest approach is to start with the middle digit, in the centre of the cab, then work outwards in either direction. It is possible to do more than one digit at the same time, which will help to check the spacing as you go.

Sometimes it might be preferable to apply the numbers from the outside in, as was the case on a 7mm scale LMS Jinty that came to me to be painted.

ADDING LETTERING AND NUMBERS, AND VARNISHING

This particular model has a five-digit number, so you need to start by placing the middle digit in the centre of the panel.

Check the height as before, measuring with dividers from a consistent point.

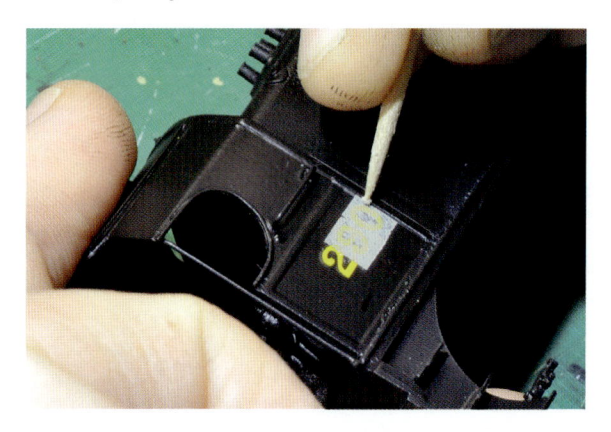

Once the centre digit is permanently in place, locate the two digits on either side, checking the spacing is equal between each of the digits as you go.

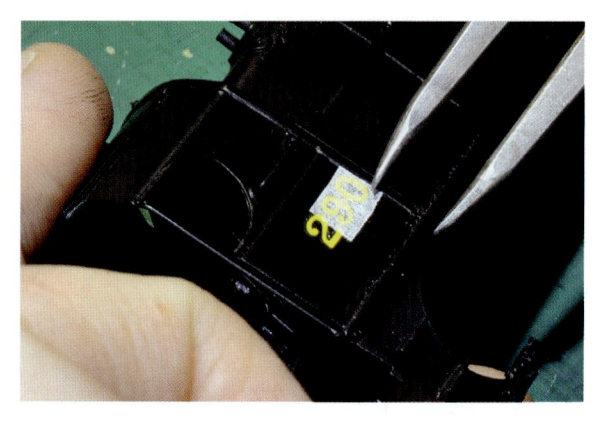

As always, make a final check on the height before soaking off the carrier film.

The space on the bunker where the numbers were to be placed looked tight for the size of number being used. All was fine, but I decided to put the outer two digits on first, ensuring that there was sufficient space in between for the remaining two digits.

These Pressfix transfers have left a slight shadow of residue after fixing. This can be removed with some white spirit and a cocktail stick, or some water and washing up liquid.

ADDING LETTERING AND NUMBERS, AND VARNISHING

Big Bertha now weathered and reassembled.

Big Bertha where she is meant to be -- pushing from behind.

The space on the bunker of a Jinty is quite tight for the numbers, so I decided to start with the outer digits.

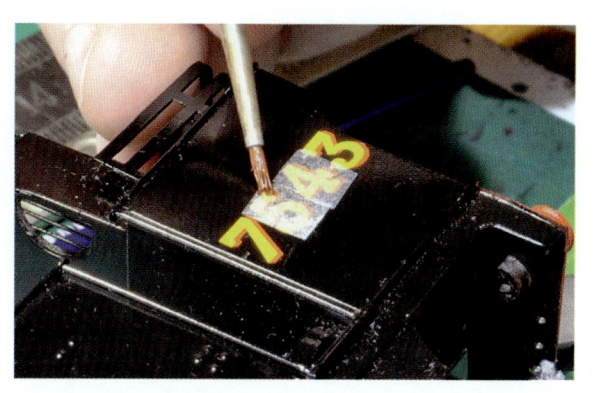

Once the outer digits were in place, it was easier to set the spacing for the inner digits. During this process, dust will be collecting on the model. This will need to be cleaned off before varnishing and weathering.

ADDING LETTERING AND NUMBERS, AND VARNISHING

The same Jinty after varnishing and some medium weathering.

With a crew added, the model takes on some character.

ADDING LETTERING AND NUMBERS, AND VARNISHING

This side of the tender has a Pressfix 'BRITISH RAILWAYS' transfer. It has been pressed into position and double-checked for alignment.

Water is dabbed on to soak off the carrier paper.

Once it has been released by the water, the carrier paper can be removed with tweezers.

Finally, the area is mopped dry by dabbing with some kitchen towel.

APPLYING METHFIX TRANSFERS

The first step when applying Methfix transfers is to mix the solution of methylated spirit and water, in the ratio of 3:1. This is applied to the model with the transfer in place, in order to activate the adhesive. Only a small amount of solution is needed – perhaps a teaspoon in total. The transfer is cut out in the same way as with Pressfix, and placed on the model. It will not stick straight away, so it can be moved around initially. If it is a large transfer, it is helpful to dampen part of it slightly with the meth solution, using a brush; this will tack it into position, but still allow its position to be adjusted. Check for alignment at each end and along the length of the transfer, then dampen further with the brush and carefully press in position. Leave it for at least ten minutes, until the meth solution has evaporated and the transfer looks dry, then apply some plain water to the carrier tissue and carefully lift it away from the transfer. If the transfer comes away too, apply more meth solution, press down, and leave it for a little longer.

Start by mixing three parts methylated spirit with one part water. Just a small amount (less than a teaspoon) is needed.

As with Pressfix, cut around the whole transfer, then slide a knife in between the carrier film and the backing paper.

To get a Methfix transfer to hold its position, place it as close as possible to where it needs to go, dampen it slightly with the methylated spirit solution using a brush, then adjust its position with a cocktail stick. As always, double-check the alignment.

ADDING LETTERING AND NUMBERS, AND VARNISHING 131

The spacing between 'Great' and 'Western' on the sheet is too large for this model, so each word had to be applied separately.

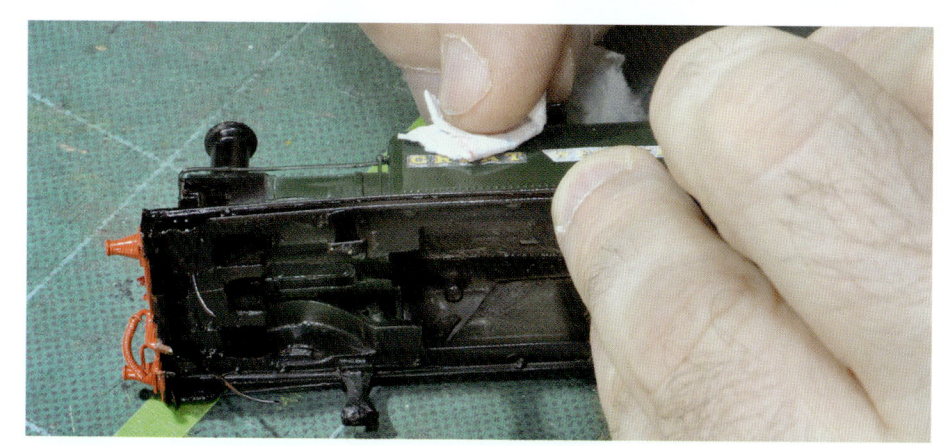

Mop up any excess solution by dabbing with a piece of kitchen towel.

After a minimum of 10 minutes, soak off the carrier paper with just water.

132 ADDING LETTERING AND NUMBERS, AND VARNISHING

Any residue from the transfer can be cleaned with a cocktail stick and some white spirit as before.

This side of the tender has a Methfix 'BRITISH RAILWAYS'. One end has been moistened with the methylated spirit solution to hold it in position whilst the rest of it is aligned.

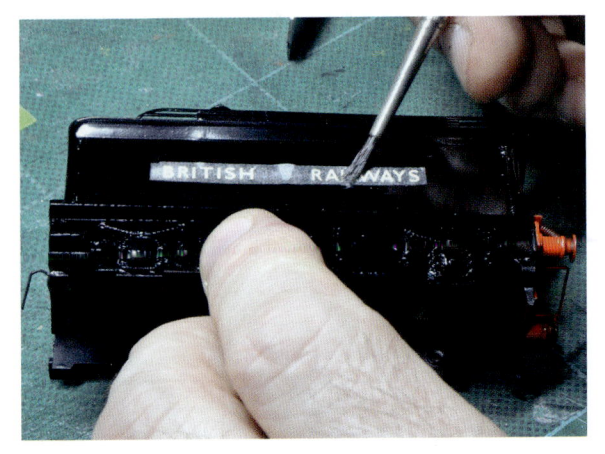

Once it is in the correct position, apply more solution with a brush, then leave it for at least 10 minutes, during which time excess solution will evaporate.

ADDING LETTERING AND NUMBERS, AND VARNISHING

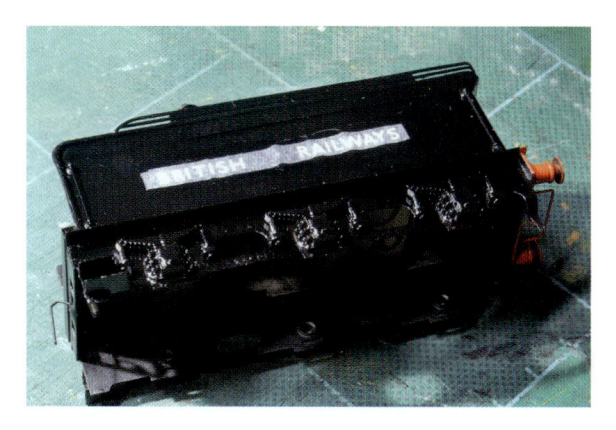

Dab on some water with a finger to soak off the carrier paper.

Once it has been separated, remove the carrier film and mop up the water.

APPLYING WATERSLIDE TRANSFERS

You can create waterslide transfers yourself, for boiler band and cylinder lining, by painting on to waterslide transfer paper (see Chapter 7). When the paint is completely dry, they are cut out, soaked in water, then carefully slid sideways off the backing paper directly on to the model.

If you want to use ready-made waterslide transfers, Fox has an extensive range, which I have used on a number of occasions. There are also a number of other suppliers of this type of transfer, covering some quite diverse railway models.

When applying waterslide transfers, it is important to note that they tend to come on carrying film, so it is necessary to cut very close to the actual transfer when cutting out. If the transfer represents lettering with significant spacing, such as 'LMS' or 'LNER', the carrying film between the letters will need to be cut away, otherwise it will be very visible on the finished model. Cutting it away before applying will mean that you lose the spacing of the letters, so you will need to reset this as you apply them to the model.

Waterslide transfers can be adjusted on the model whilst wet. If they have begun to dry, they can be loosened and adjusted further with some more water, or some Micro Set if they are slightly dryer. However, if they are completely dry, damage will occur if you try to adjust them.

APPLYING RUB-DOWN TRANSFERS

Rub-down transfers come with a carrying film on the front of the transfer. Place this film on the model so that the actual transfer is in the correct position, then attach with some tape. Rub the film over the area that is covering the transfer with a firm blunt object, such as the handle of a craft knife, or a blunted cocktail stick for small areas, then slowly lift the film. If any of the transfer has not taken, reposition and rub again. If necessary, any gaps that occur due to the transfer breaking can be filled in with paint.

This is not my preferred type of transfer, as a disappointing amount of transfer often has to be painted back in after application. However, it is usually possible to achieve the desired effect afterwards.

HAND-PAINTING

MAKING AMENDMENTS AND ADAPTATIONS

Having had a go at hand-painting letters and numbers on a Private Owner coal wagon and on my Wantage Tramway No 5 (see later this chapter) a number of years ago, I have worked more recently on two examples that involved a degree of hand-painting in order to amend existing work.

ADDING LETTERING AND NUMBERS, AND VARNISHING

On the gauge 2 LNWR Precursor tank locomotive (see also Chapter 5), the letters had been applied, but something did not look right. On closer examination, it became apparent that the letter 'L' was not at a true right angle. The bottom of the letter was truly aligned horizontally, but the vertical element was leaning backwards. As I had no spare letters (the letters were rather old, and had been provided specifically for the task), I decided to amend the letter by hand. First, the left-hand edge of the vertical part of the 'L' was straightened by painting a black line with the bow pen. The gold on the right-hand side now needed to be made parallel, and this was again done using the bow pen. Finally, the red shading needed to be adjusted, using the same method.

When I was recently presented with an ex-LNER D3 to paint, I was given a photograph of the prototype, which showed that the first digit, a '6', was not standard for that livery. A standard BR '6' has a very slight curve to the diagonally upward tail, but the photograph showed a fully rounded upward tail on this '6'. The owner of the model asked me to replicate this different style of digit.

After the standard British Railways '6' digit had been applied and left to dry, the top section was removed by cutting with a craft knife, and scraping gently with a cocktail stick.

This letter was not set exactly at a right angle. Whilst the base was level, the vertical part was leaning backwards. As a replacement was not available, it had to be straightened. First, a black line was painted with a bow pen up the left-hand edge to straighten this side, then a gold line was painted up the right-hand side, to make the gold section parallel again. Finally, the red shading was adjusted in the same way as the gold.

Mixing some gloss white and gloss yellow (Humbrol 7) together in the ratio of 1:1 produced a perfect match for the colour of the transfer.

ADDING LETTERING AND NUMBERS, AND VARNISHING | 135

The upward curve was formed in one sweep with a lining brush.

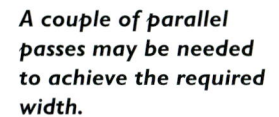

A couple of parallel passes may be needed to achieve the required width.

After a few minutes' drying time, brush along the edge of the paint with a clean brush dampened with white spirit, to thin and tidy it as necessary.

136 ADDING LETTERING AND NUMBERS, AND VARNISHING

The finished number, after varnishing and some light weathering.

This is how the standard British Railways '6' appears.

I started by applying a standard number '6' from a sheet of Methfix. Once it was fully dry, I cut off and removed the upward tail, so only the circular part remained. The colour of the number is cream, so I mixed a small amount of white paint with a small amount of yellow (Humbrol no. 7). Then, with one of my lining brushes, I formed the curved upward tail. The adjacent numbers provided a guide as to the correct height. After the paint had had a few

The finished model – and the number looks quite at home.

ADDING LETTERING AND NUMBERS, AND VARNISHING 137

ABOVE: **Both sides were given the same treatment.**

BELOW: **The loco at home on its layout.**

138 ADDING LETTERING AND NUMBERS, AND VARNISHING

The hand-painted '18', having used the Letraset numbers as a guide.

minutes to start to go tacky, the edges of the curve could be tidied and thinned to match the rest of the number.

When it came to numbering the Midland and South Western Junction Railway locomotive seen earlier in this book (*see* Chapter 5), as '18', no specific transfer was available and photographic evidence was very sparse. However, although the M&SWJR logo had been specially made to order, the font of the numbers used by the company was similar to one that is available in Letraset rub-down transfers. An appropriate size was obtained, albeit in white, and the digits were applied separately.

Once the numbers had been placed in the correct position and rubbed down, the next step was to paint over the white with gold lining paint from Precision Paints. For this, I used one of my front-line brushes that are normally reserved for lining. The edges were then tidied up with a small amount of white spirit on a clean brush, in the same way as for cleaning up lining (*see* Chapter 7).

HAND LETTERING FROM SCRATCH

Part of this process may bring back memories of school days. Start by drawing the lettering or numbers on to tracing paper with a very fine pencil, then rub the back of the tracing paper with a softer leaded pencil. Place the tracing paper right side up in the position of the lettering, and trace over the lettering with the fine pencil. The result will be a faint outline on the surface of the model. I find it useful to include horizontal lines top and bottom of the lettering, so that the upper and lower limit can be seen when painting.

When you are ready to do the painting, start with the straight lines, applying the paint with a bow pen, then paint in any curves and fill in any gaps with a lining brush. Allow it to dry for a few minutes, then move on to the tidying-up process. Use a clean brush moistened with white spirit, then blotted on kitchen towel, and draw it around the edge of any curves that are not smooth. You will see the edge become neater.

ADDING LETTERING AND NUMBERS, AND VARNISHING

To ensure that the ends of the letters are correct, draw the brush across them. This will take away any excess paint, leaving nice, tidy right-angled edges.

If the letters need shading, this can be applied 24 hours after the letters themselves. Take the same approach as before: straight lines first with a bow pen, curves with a brush next, then tidying up a little later.

RIGHT: **Painted some 15 years ago, an early attempt at hand-lettering in 7mm scale.**

The desired lettering is drawn on to some tracing paper with a fine pencil. The horizontal lines top and bottom are helpful at both the drawing stage and the painting stage.

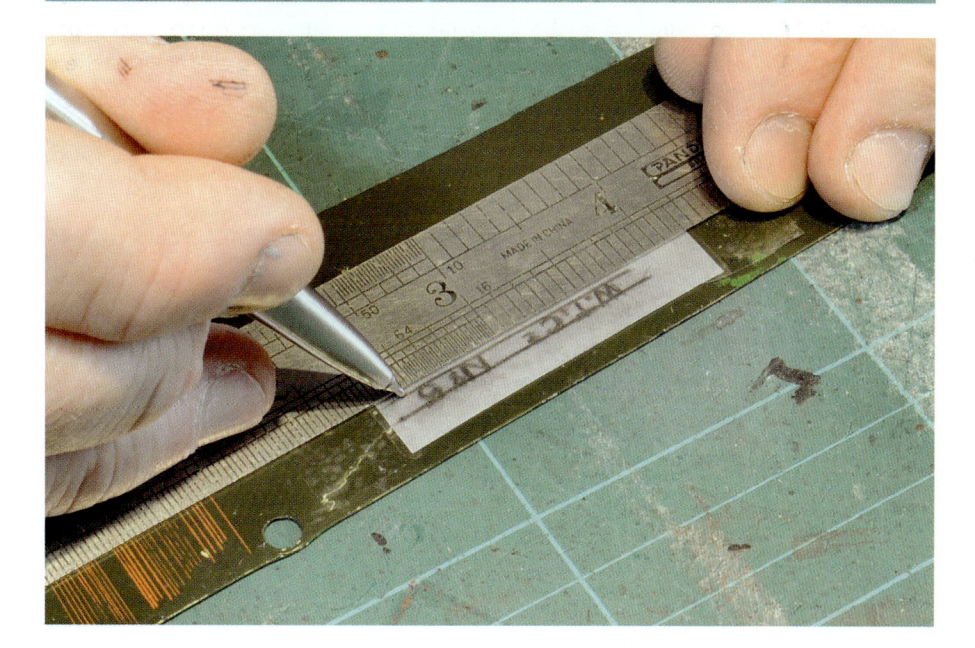

Having rubbed the back with pencil (with a soft lead if possible), the lettering is traced straight on to the painted surface of the model.

140 ADDING LETTERING AND NUMBERS, AND VARNISHING

Start by painting the straight lines with a bow pen straight on to the traced image. The pencil marks are very difficult to see in anything other than very good light.

The curved letters are then painted in with a lining brush.

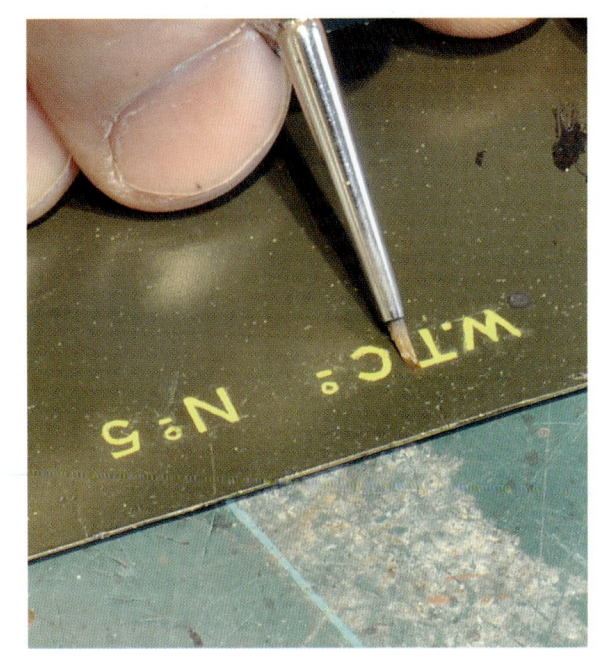

Once the paint is on, any tidying can be carried out, using a brush moistened with white spirit. Ensure that the ends of the letters are squared off, by drawing the brush along the edge.

Drawing the same brush around the curves will smooth off any irregularities in the edge of the letter.

ADDING LETTERING AND NUMBERS, AND VARNISHING | 141

To apply the shading, start with the straight lines, using a bow pen.

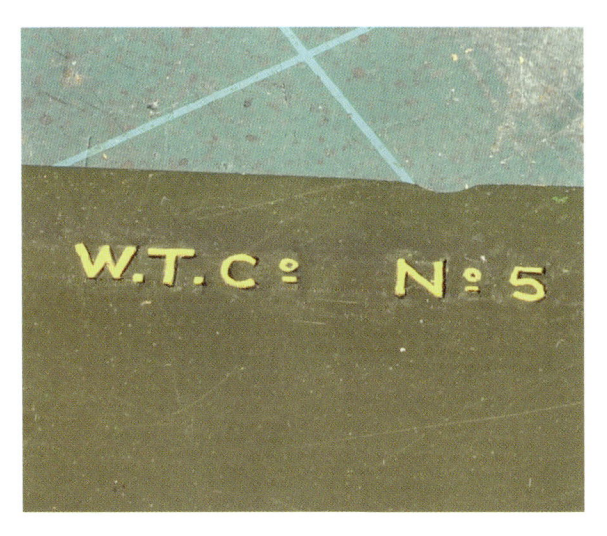

The final result.

VARNISHING

If a model is to be left unweathered, varnishing is the last stage. It is an important part of the process and perhaps the most stressful. You are about to spray something over the whole of the model that you have just spent a great deal of time painting, lining, and enhancing with the application of transfers. If something goes wrong at this stage, in the worst-case scenario the model may need to be stripped back to bare metal, and the whole process started again. Also, this is an ideal opportunity for any dust that has found its way on to the surface of the model to become permanently attached to it underneath the varnish.

There are a variety of varnishes around. In years gone by, I have used Humbrol acrylic satin and matt varnishes, and Humbrol and Precision Paints enamel-based varnish. These days, I tend to use one of two options. For a satin finish, I use Ronseal gloss varnish (not the water-soluble version), with a few drops of Precision Paints matting agent stirred into it. Using my mixing dessert spoon, I measure out about half a spoon of varnish and three drops of matting agent. This is then thinned with the same amount of white spirit. For a matt finish, I use Testors Dullcote, which I thin with turps in the ratio of 1:1.

My preferred varnishes: Ronseal gloss with some Phoenix Precision matting agent for satin finishes, and Testors Dullcote with turps for matt finishes.

ADDING LETTERING AND NUMBERS, AND VARNISHING

After lettering, the Great Western 514 is given a thin coat of the Ronseal varnish to take down the gloss.

This ex-Southern Railway O2 has had a coat of Testors Dullcote.

ADDING LETTERING AND NUMBERS, AND VARNISHING 143

After the first application of Dullcote, more can be applied within minutes to achieve the required level of matting down.

Needless to say, with either option, it is well worth spending time on spraying varnish on to your painted test piece of metal, to see the effect it has. This will help you to get used to how much or how little needs to be sprayed, how much can be sprayed before problems arise, and what happens when too much varnish is sprayed.

Spraying the Ronseal mix is not difficult, but it needs to be done with great care, as it takes a while to dry, on a par with sprayed enamels. Unlike when spraying paint, this needs to be carefully misted on to the model from a distance of no closer than 5cm. A very light coat is all that is needed. A heavier coat will end up rather shiny and inclined to form

One of three Great Western Castles that passed through my hands recently. This one was to be painted in close to ex-works condition, so it received a Ronseal varnish and no weathering.

144 ADDING LETTERING AND NUMBERS, AND VARNISHING

runs. As it is sprayed, you will notice the gloss finish reduce down to a satin.

I approach spraying the Dullcote in the same way as spraying the Ronseal varnish, but this dries very much more quickly and also can be built up rather more. The more matt you want the finish, the more Dullcote you spray. I have on occasion achieved a desired level of satin by using the Dullcote.

Whichever route you take for varnishing, practise first. Try your varnish on a test piece, then make sure the model is completely free from dust before you start to spray, and take your time.

Just a very light coat of Ronseal is required; the level of gloss quickly diminishes as the varnish goes on.

It is important to pick out piping detail in the painting process.

CHAPTER NINE

WEATHERING

It is fair to say that a book on painting is not complete if the topic of weathering is not covered. However, it is equally fair to say that the subject of weathering is large enough to warrant its own book, and such books do exist. There are also professional model-makers who specialize in providing a weathering service.

It is fascinating to watch a model come to life with each stage of the painting process. Not every model has to be weathered – I have painted models that I would prefer to have left alone after the varnishing stage, but the client specifically requested weathering – but the majority of models do benefit from some weathering, no matter how light. In real life, even a recently cleaned vehicle can have corners or pockets of dirt and grime.

Weathering falls into one of two categories. The first is a simple toning down of the model following painting. I am quite frequently asked to apply a toning-down wash to a new ready-to-run model. The second is weathering with a capital 'W'. In either case, reference to colour photographs of the prototype is essential to achieve a realistic finish. There are a number of books of the steam era with colour photos available.

The range of weathering products has grown enormously in recent years, with washes, powders and pigments, as well as all the weathering-specific colours of enamel and acrylic paints.

SIMPLE TONING DOWN

Although it needs to be done with care (it is not just a case of waving the airbrush in front of the model), a simple toning down can be done relatively quickly. For a model that is viewed from a distance, or one that passes by at speed, this approach can be very effective. Quite often I am asked to apply a toning-down coat after painting and varnishing a model, just to give it the look of a 'locomotive in use'. The amount of the toning that is applied can be varied, as can the shades of paint used.

My simple toning weathering wash generally consists of two out of three colours: Brown (Revell no. 84), plus either Matt Black (Revell no. 8 or Humbrol no. 33) or Metalcote Gunmetal (Humbrol

A ready-to-run Patriot, straight from the box. The lining is rather bright and the plastic body has a particular sheen to it.

WEATHERING

The Patriot has been renumbered and a light weathering wash has been applied.

A similarly bright ready-to-run Jubilee.

Like the Patriot, the Jubilee has been renumbered and the same weathering wash has been applied.

WEATHERING 147

The D16 in as-new condition.

The weathering has taken the glare out of the lining and softened the overall colour.

This A3 has had a light weathering wash after varnishing.

The B17 has had a slightly heavier weathering wash, what I would call 'medium'.

no. 27004). If the model is black, I use the Gunmetal, as this paint contains metal particles that can be polished up once the paint is dry to lift the black of the model and bring life to its appearance. If the model is any other colour, I use matt black. I start with a mix of one part brown to two parts black or Gunmetal, then I add an equal amount of white spirit, so the mix is 50:50 paint to thinners.

As always, it is important to spray with the airbrush on to the test sheet to check the flow, and also to remind yourself of how much trigger is needed. You only need a minimal amount of paint flow, so little in fact that at first you will think that there is no paint flowing. I often point the airbrush to my glove, just to check that paint is being sprayed. When spraying a toning wash on to a model, I will generally be spraying from a much greater distance than usual, perhaps 10cm from the model. Only if I am working on spraying some weathering into tight corners will I move in closer. The approach is several light passes with the airbrush, looking closely at the model throughout, to see the tone building up until the desired level is achieved.

The paint mix can be varied for different areas of

WEATHERING

the model, but more of this where we look at more complex weathering projects.

DETAILED WEATHERING

Modelling colleagues who focus on military models have developed the skills of weathering much further than those who concentrate on model railways. This is possibly due to the purely visual nature of their models, which do not have the added dimension of movement, as the railways do. Because of the interest in military models, the number of weathering products has grown exponentially in recent years, and this is having an effect on the options for railway modellers.

With such a wide range of products available, how should you make your choices? Fortunately, one of the experts in the field has selected 16 of the most useful weathering products for railway modelling (there were just too many to fit into a top ten), and these have been packaged together by Phil Atkinson of Hobby Holidays. Included are some enamel paints, acrylic paints and pigments, along with a couple of pages of instructions, which detail what each of the products are suited to, and how to use them.

The tools I use for weathering are my Iwata airbrush and a variety of brushes. Weathering can be hard on brushes, so I use old ones that are past their best, along with some cheaper ones.

Before getting started on the model, it is important to have some photos to hand, ideally in colour, so that you have something to follow and an idea of what it should look like when you finish. It is easy to overdo weathering, so the best approach is to do a bit, then put it aside, and review it later with fresh eyes. It is easy to apply more weathering, but difficult if not impossible to take it off.

I will normally start with the body, giving it a weathering spray. Starting as a base with my standard toning mix (mentioned earlier in this chapter), I will give the model a spray over, but I am not aiming for an even coating this time. I may vary the paint mix slightly, then spray a little more, with slightly more black further up the model, and slightly more brown further down, around the rear, and on tender frames.

It is worth including some Humbrol Metalcote Gunmetal paint in the mix, as it has another dimension to it. Once it has dried, the metal component in this paint can be polished up with a cotton bud or a brush.

This box of tricks, put together by Hobby Holidays, is an ideal starting place when it comes to weathering products.

A variety of enamels, acrylics and pigments, together with a description of each one, and a suggestion of how to use it.

My collection of brushes: the best brushes for any detail or general painting; the older and cheaper brushes for dry-brushing, pigments, and other weathering applications.

WEATHERING

Next, apply some weathering powders. Think about using black on the top of the boiler, firebox and cab for soot, perhaps some rust on the smokebox, and something lighter underneath the smokebox to represent ash.

DRY-BRUSHING

Some areas such as tender frames could benefit from further colour variation by dry-brushing. Put a drop of a couple of shades of brown, such as Leather and Underframe Dirt, on to the palette without mixing them together. Pick up a small amount of each colour on the brush, mix them elsewhere on the palette, wipe the brush on some kitchen towel so that the brush is almost dry, then take it to the model. Dry-brushing is effectively dragging the almost dry brush on the surface to be painted, so that only a small amount of paint is applied, thus creating more subtle tones.

If enamel paints have been used in the spraying mix, they can be revisited quite a few hours after spraying, with a brush moistened with white spirit. Streaking effects can be created in this way, simulating the way in which the weather will partly wash down vertical faces.

Interesting effects can be created on buffer beams too, using the same principle. Soon after spraying, apply a small amount of white spirit with a brush to loosen some of the paint, and work it into the corners between the buffer beam and the buffer shanks, and around the rivets. If the result looks a little too extreme, a little more weathering mix can be sprayed on.

METAL BLACKS

There are various metal blacking fluids available, which chemically blacken the surface of the metal, as an alternative to applying a coat of paint. I have an old bottle of Casey's Gun Blue, which will turn brass and nickel silver to a brown shade. The metal must be completely clean before applying – a scrub with a fibreglass pencil will help. As soon as it is applied, you will see it start to work. When you are happy with the amount of toning, wash it off with water to stop the process.

PRACTICAL EXAMPLES OF WEATHERING

Lets now take a look at some various projects as they undergo the weathering process. First, there is a 4mm scale O2.

This 4mm scale O2 is about to have a full weathering job.

152 WEATHERING

Starting with a mix of brown and Metalcote Gunmetal as before, spray around the front of the O2 and then work up the sides.

Work up the other side of the O2 as well.

Add a little matt black to the mix for the upper part of the body.

WEATHERING | 153

Do not forget the chassis, particularly the cylinders.

Give the tender body a treatment similar to that on the sides of the loco.

Add a little more brown for the tender frames.

WEATHERING

Use the same mix with a little more brown for the buffer beams and tender rear.

Once it is dry, the Metalcote can be polished.

With an old brush, polish in a vertical direction. With just a few light strokes, the metal component will start to shine slightly.

WEATHERING

The next stage is to introduce some weathering powders, more recently referred to as 'pigments'. My 'Rust and Coal Dust' selection was originally sold by Carrs and has lasted quite a long time.

Using an old brush, bring some of the black powder to the model.

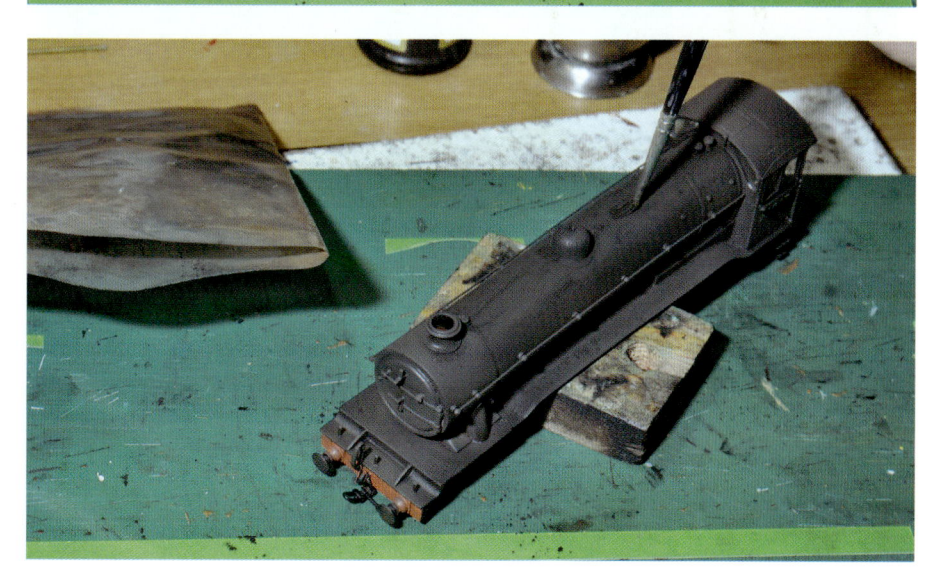

Work the powder into the paint surface. Just a little gentle scrubbing is required.

WEATHERING

Wipe the majority of the paint off the brush with some kitchen towel, so that only a little paint remains.

Drag the brush along the surface, to distribute a small amount of paint.

Build up the paint until you achieve the effect that you want.

WEATHERING | 159

The finished model. Some matt white paint has been dry-brushed down from the firebox wash-out plugs.

The weathered model looks quite at home on the layout.

A view from the other side on the layout.

WEATHERING

The next project is a 7mm scale WD. This model is slightly unusual, in that the chassis is permanently fixed to the body, which made it slightly harder to work on, in that it was more awkward to hold than putting your fingers inside the boiler.

This 7mm scale WD is ready for some weathering. The chassis has had some treatment already and, unusually, does not separate from the body.

Start off with the brown/Metalcote Gunmetal wash.

WEATHERING | 161

Ensure that you get into the corners.

My approach with colours is to use slightly more brown further down, and more black on top.

The tender is given similar treatment.

162 WEATHERING

In 7mm scale, it is easier to get into some of the corners.

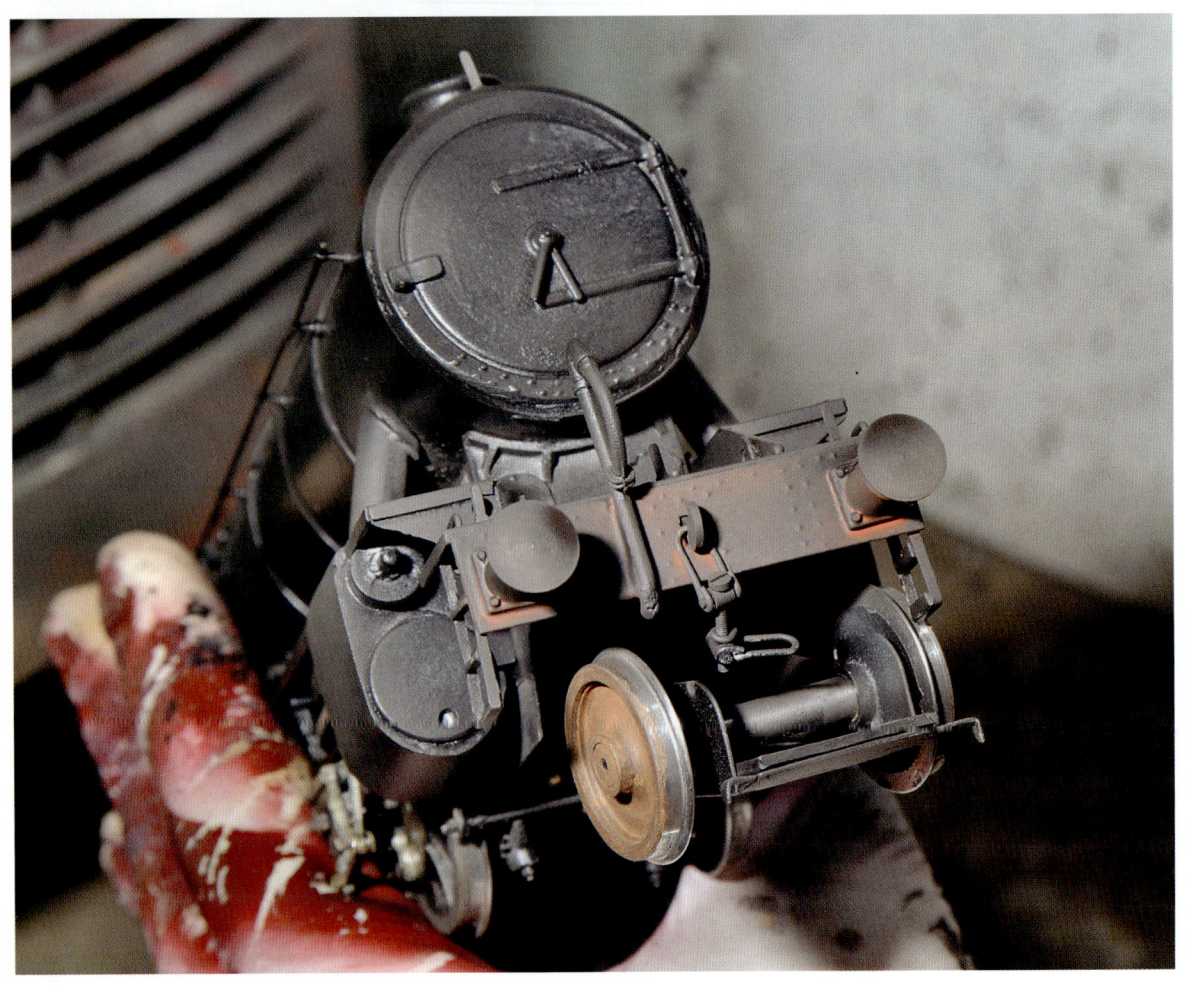

The buffer beam has had a coat of weathering, but it has not gone right into the corners.

WEATHERING | 163

Moisten a brush with white spirit (this time not blotted on kitchen towel), and then put it on the buffer beam.

Work the brush to loosen the paint.

WEATHERING

Work some of the paint into the corner between the buffer shank and the buffer beam, then leave it to dry over for a little while. You have a number of hours to go back to it and loosen it again with white spirit if you are not happy with it.

Now a slightly blacker shade is applied to the upper parts.

WEATHERING | 165

Apply the paint sparingly; it is a lot easier to add more than to take it off.

A browner shade is applied to the lower part of the tender.

166 WEATHERING

When weathering, it is vitally important to do a bit, let it dry, then review how it looks, comparing it to photos of the real thing.

More underframe weathering going on.

WEATHERING

Now back to the loco, and check under the boiler.

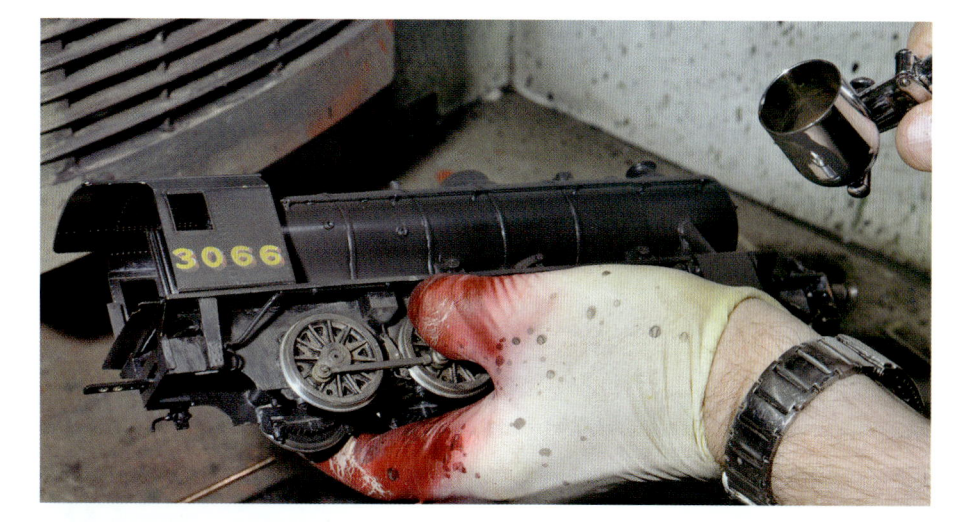

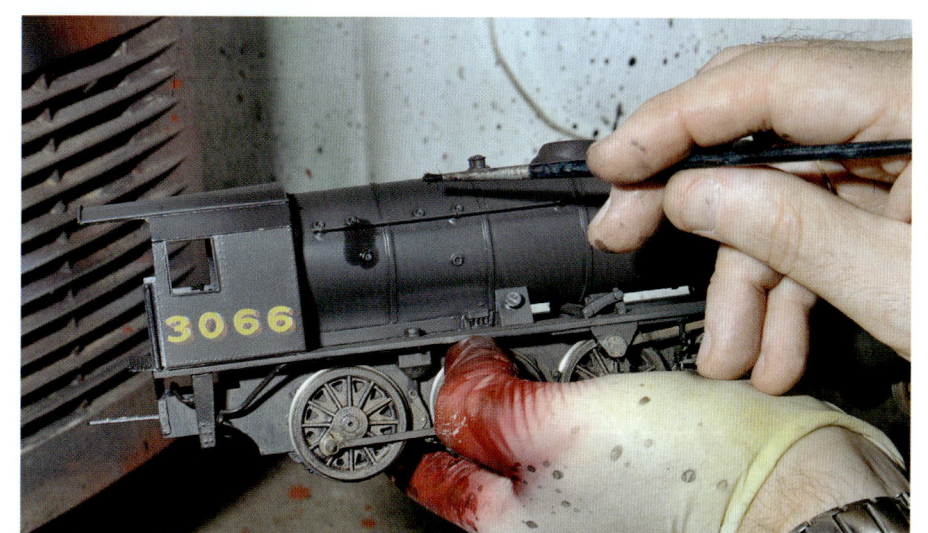

A little white spirit is added to apply some streaking.

It is worth using each paint mix for the appropriate areas on both the loco and tender, before changing the shade slightly for the next area. This also gives the paint you have just put on a little time to dry slightly, so you can look at the overall shade more accurately.

170 WEATHERING

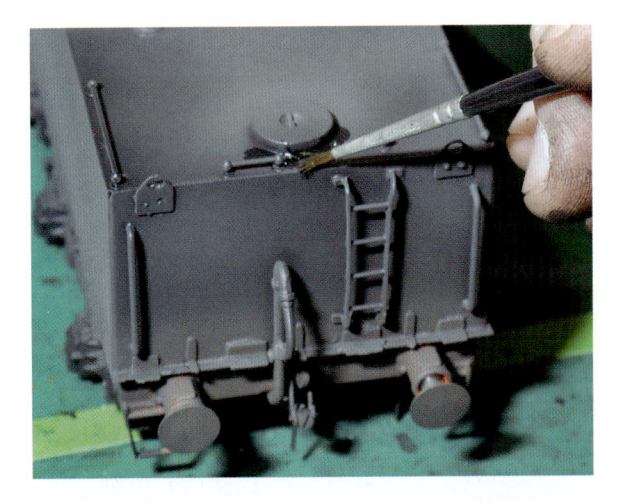

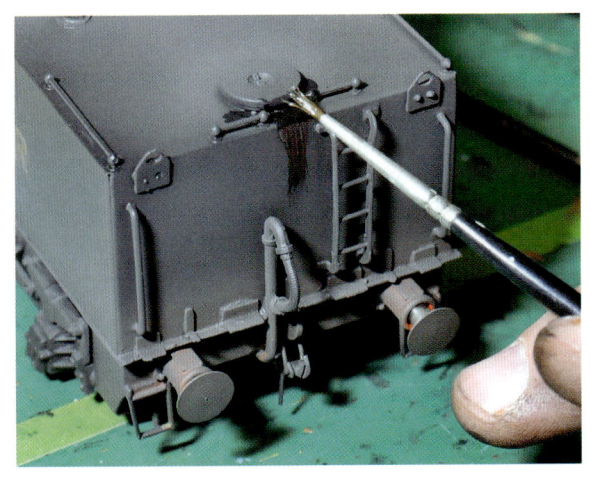

TOP LEFT: **The Murky Water is simply brushed on, like any other paint.**

TOP RIGHT: **Build it up until you have the desired effect.**

LEFT: **Allow it to dry off a little, review the effect, and then add a little more if needed.**

The finished model.

WEATHERING

The ash underneath the firebox door is another product from the Hobby Holidays box of tricks.

RIGHT: **The tender closely reflected the photograph that I had been given as a guide for the model.**

The owner of the model particularly liked the water effect.

A view showing the variety of shades, and their intensity on the buffer beam.

WEATHERING

Another angle on the buffer beam.

Staying in 7mm scale, the next project consists of two Dapol Jinties. I decided to add one of these into my collection, and a friend did the same. The sequence starts with the two models more or less straight from the box, although the LMS model had been renumbered before it came to me.

Two 7mm scale Dapol Jinties came my way recently for weathering. The BR-liveried model is mine and the LMS belonged to a friend. He had renumbered it and some residue from this process was evident on the bunker. This was removed with some white spirit, but would disappear under the weathering in any case.

The Jinty bodies were treated to a spraying of varying shades. The morning after the previous afternoon's spraying, I took a flat brush moistened slightly with white spirit, then streaked it vertically down the tanks and the bunker. The sprayed paint had dried, but it had not fully hardened, so it could be brought back.

The effect sought after was that which occurs as the weather washes down the built-up weathering. As always, it is important to allow time for it to dry over. After reviewing it, I decided to tone down the streaking on the LMS body slightly by applying another light weathering wash with the airbrush.

WEATHERING

The dry-brushing mix was prepared in the palette, this time with some Humbrol 53 Gunmetal added. Small amounts of this can be mixed in, but I will use this on the wheels.

Apply the dry-brushing to the frames.

It is important not to forget the area behind the wheels. If the wheel sets cannot be removed easily, it will have to be done through the spokes.

WEATHERING

Painting through the spokes will inevitably result in some paint on the wheels, but this can be dealt with after the frames. Humbrol 53 Gunmetal was dry-brushed on to the wheels, using a radial motion, as any deposits on the real thing would move outwards due to the centrifugal force whilst in motion.

The jars of medium and dark rust pigments (right) are from the Hobby Holidays box of tricks, but the Pigment Fixer is not.

A little of each of the pigment shades is applied to the brake gear.

Coupling rods may be treated in a couple of different ways. Here, they are being chemically blackened.

WEATHERING

The other solution for coupling rods and valve gear is a mix of Humbrol 27003 Metalcote Polished Steel and Humbrol 9 Gloss Tan, mixed 1:1.

The Metalcote and Gloss Tan mix is then brushed on to the rods. Once it is fully dried, it can be polished up with a cotton bud. The effect is of oily steel.

Keep reviewing the progress so far.

WEATHERING | 177

The brake pull rods are made of a different plastic from the rest of the brake gear. It is shinier, and the pigments would not remain in place, so this was a job for the Pigment Fixer.

Despite what the instructions said, I decided to apply the fixer first.

Work in some pigments.

Mix in a bit of both shades.

WEATHERING | 179

The two finished locomotives.

PLANKING

Some vehicles, wagons and older coaches have sides with visible planking. Dirt can collect in the gaps, and this can be reflected on the model. I put a small amount of white spirit in the bottom of an egg cup, then put a drop of paint on the side. Pick up a bit of paint on the brush, then dip into the white spirit. Place the brush on the planking and allow a small amount of paint to run down the gap between the planks. Work it in if necessary with the brush, then wipe over the planks lightly with a kitchen towel moistened with white spirit.

Something a little more unusual: Welsh Highland Railway coaches made by my brother Ivan, who models in narrow gauge in both 4mm and 7mm scales.

WEATHERING

The planking is particularly noticeable on these models. In real life, dirt collects between the planking and is often left behind when the rest of the surface is cleaned.

LEFT: **Some medium brown enamel is put on to the side of an egg cup, with some white spirit at the bottom. For this method, the paint needs to flow.**

BELOW LEFT: **With some paint on the brush, dip it into the white spirit then place it on to the planking. The paint will flow down the planking gap. If necessary, work it down a little with the brush.**

BELOW RIGHT: **Wipe off the excess paint that is on the surface of the planks with some kitchen towel moistened with white spirit.**

WEATHERING 181

The planking gaps after weathering.

A 7mm coal wagon weathered by Barry Norman, using techniques similar to those described here.

The underside of the coal wagon.

This 7mm scale Q6 is another example of the results that can be achieved using these methods of weathering.

A view of the other side of the Q6.

CLEANING UP

After use, brushes need to be cleaned to maximize their life. My front-line brushes, and particularly my lining brushes, have lasted for a number of years, and this is very much down to taking care of them after use. First, as soon as I have finished with a brush, I dip it into my bottle of dirty white spirit, to get rid of most of the paint. At the end of every modelling session, all brushes that have come into contact with paint get a wash. I dip each brush into my artist's brush cleaner, then work them in on the hand, before washing off in water. Finally, I do a quick check of the brush to ensure that all the bristles are pointing in the right direction. If not, a pinch between the fingers will normally correct this.

Painting models is very rewarding as soon your model is touched by colour, you will see it begin to come to life. While lining is perhaps the most exacting stage, weathering is probably the most creative, requiring a more artistic approach. The best way to improve your skills and creativity is to read articles and books on the subject, then practise and adapt the advice until you are comfortable with the methods. Over the years, you will probably have to resort to using a certain amount of paint stripper to correct any mistakes, but it is all part of the learning process. If you are happy using an airbrush, with some practice and advice there is great satisfaction to be had from creating neat lines and nice tidy corners. Hopefully, this book will give you the confidence to give it a try, and the advice you need to help you to improve your skills. Happy painting!

Close-up of the GWR steam railmotor.

The GWR railmotor was given a very light spray over of weathering mix, just to take the tone down slightly. This process really brought the model to life.

The G1 seen earlier needed a more matt finish, so Dullcote was used at the varnishing stage.

The G1 also had a very light spray over of weathering mix.

WEATHERING | 185

Another of the trio of 4mm scale Castles.

This Castle had a light spray of weathering mix.

The owner of the third Castle asked for medium weathering, so this one is ever so slightly dirtier.

WEATHERING

It is important to look after your brushes. After every use, my brushes get a wash in some old white spirit to remove the excess paint.

After washing in white spirit, some artist's brush cleaner is applied.

Work the artist's brush cleaner into the brush. (This is an old brush; with my better brushes, the working in is done at a much gentler angle, to preserve the point.)

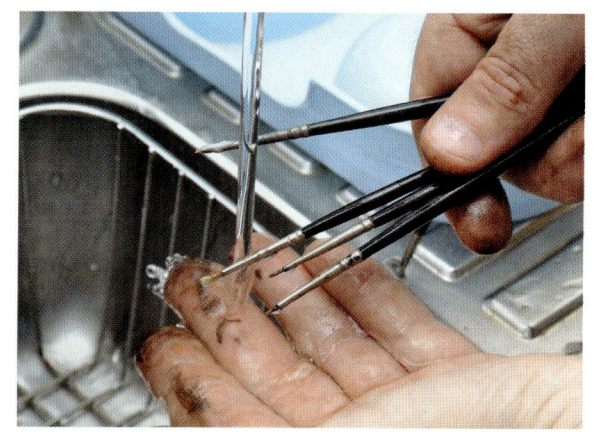

Finally, the brushes are rinsed off under water, and allowed to dry.

BIBLIOGRAPHY

Trainspotting (AK Interactive)
A more recent publication, linked to their extensive range, with a large number of photographs to illustrate various weathering techniques

Rathbone, Ian, *A Modeller's Handbook of Painting and Lining* (Wild Swan Publications)
The book from which I refined my craft, and a valuable source of reference to which I still return regularly

Welch, Martyn, *The Art of Weathering* (Wild Swan Publications)
The bible when it comes to weathering. A regular point of reference for me

SUPPLIERS

Hobby Holidays, The Spinney, Low Street, Beckingham, Doncaster, DN10 4PW
http://www.hobbyholidays.co.uk
Modelling and painting supplies, including an extensive range of weathering products

Eileen's Emporium, Highnam Business Centre, Newent Rd, Highnam, Gloucester, GL2 8DN
https://eileensemporium.com
Modelling supplies, and airbrushes

The Craft Light Company, 32 Gunton Church Lane, Lowestoft NR32 4LF
https://www.craftlights.co.uk
An extensive range of lights of very high quality

INDEX

3D-printed see composite materials
air pressure 28
airbrush
   choosing 26–7
beaded coaches 82–6
boiler bands see lining
brush-painting see painting
changing colour 47
cleaning up 182–3
composite materials 57–61
   3D-printed 60
   early GWR coaches 57–9
curves, valances and splashers see lining
dismantling coaches 14–16
dividers 68
dry-brushing see weathering
GWR Castle 21–3
filler 54–5
flush-sided coaches 86–8
hand-painting 133–8
   hand lettering from scratch 138–41
inset lining see lining
lining 12–13, 76
   boiler bands 99–102
   border lining 94–9
   coaches 82–88
   curves, valances and splashers 93–4
   difficult areas 103
   inset lining 89–93
   locomotives 89–120
   styles 76–9
   tidying 93
LMS Duchess of Sutherland 18–20
locomotives
   body 17
   case studies 18–23

chassis 16–17
magnifying visor 68
masking 44–9
   wheels 50
paint strippers 64–5
painting 23–5, 33
   brush-painting 50–2
   cellulose paints 34
   difficult areas 40
   mixing paints 35–7
   paint types 33–4
   teak-effect 61–3
   thickness 71
   top coat 40
   wheels 49
pens
   Bob Moore 70
   bow 66, 70–5
   Rotring 68
planking 179–81
spraying 9–12, 28–31, 37–44
   distance 28
thinners 27–8, 34
transfers 79–81, 121–33
   Methfix 130–2
   Pressfix 122–9
   rub-down 133
   waterslide 133
varnishing 131 141–4
Wantage Tramway Number 5 18
weathering 13, 145
   detailed 149–51
   dry-brushing 151
   metal blacks 151
   toning down 145–9

RELATED TITLES FROM CROWOOD

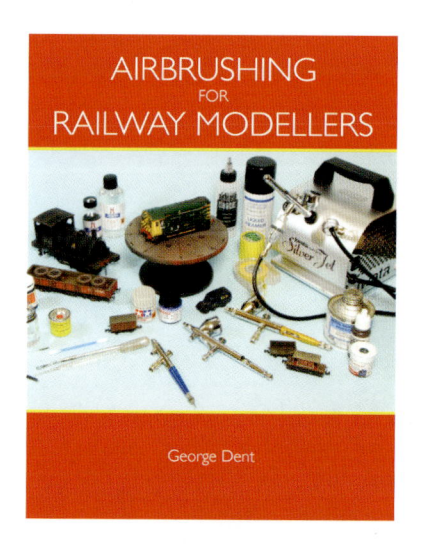

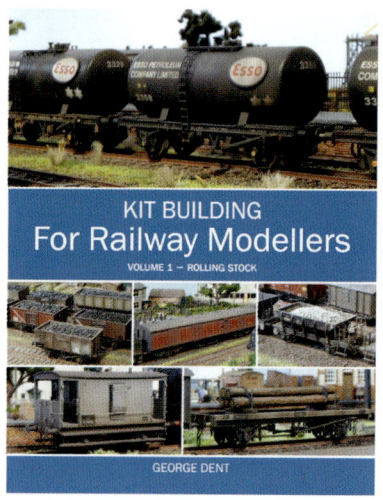

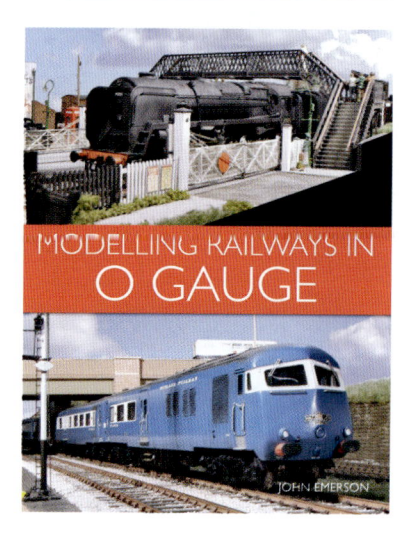

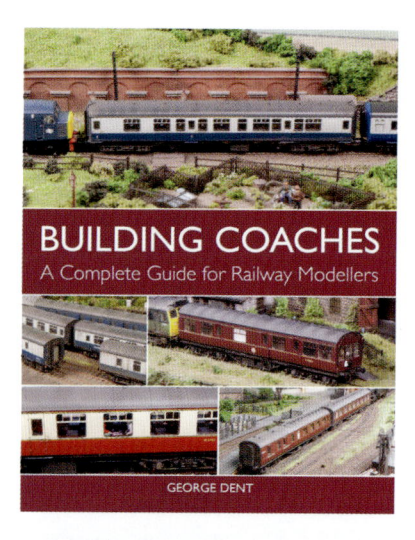

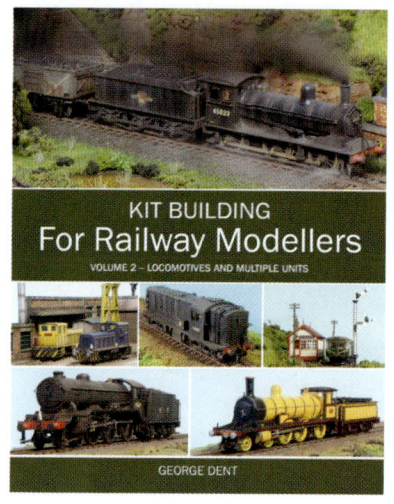

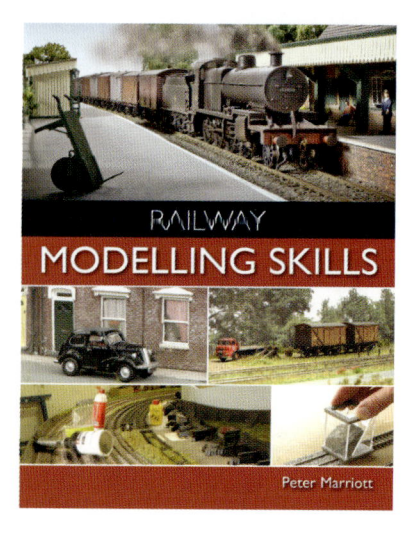

AIRBRUSHING FOR RAILWAY MODELLERS
George Dent

BUILDING COACHES
A Complete Guide for Railway Modellers
GEORGE DENT

KIT BUILDING For Railway Modellers
VOLUME 1 – ROLLING STOCK
GEORGE DENT

KIT BUILDING For Railway Modellers
VOLUME 2 – LOCOMOTIVES AND MULTIPLE UNITS
GEORGE DENT

MODELLING RAILWAYS IN O GAUGE
JOHN EMERSON

RAILWAY MODELLING SKILLS
Peter Marriott